£3·49   Gift Aid item

C000294846

FRAN ABRAMS is an investigative journalist and auon the staff of various national newspapers inclu
Telegraph and the Sunday Times. She now makes a
File on Four programme and writes for the Gu
has written five books, the most recent of which i
British Childhood, published by Atlantic Books. (
Manchester, she lives in Suffolk.

MELISSA BENN is a writer, broadcaster and campaigner. She was educated at Holland Park comprehensive and the London School of Economics where she graduated with a first in history. She has written seven books, including two novels, and has been widely published as an essayist and journalist, particularly in the *Guardian* and the *New Statesman*. She is active in the movement for comprehensive education and is currently Chair of Comprehensive Future, a parliamentary based group lobbying for fair admissions in all schools, and a Vice President of the Socialist Education Association. In 2014 she became co-Honorary President of the Keir Hardie Society.

PAULINE BRYAN has worked for both the ILP and the Fabian Society. She is a member of the Scottish Labour Campaign for Socialism, and Convenor of the Red Paper Collective. She co-edited *Class, Nation and Socialism: The Red Paper on Scotland 2014*, and contributed to *The Red Paper on Scotland 2005*, *Scotland's Road to Socialism: Time to Choose* and *A Modest Proposal: For the Agreement of the People*. She is a member of the Keir Hardie Society.

JOHN CALLOW is a Political Officer with the GMB trade union. He gained a first class honours degree at Lancaster University, an MA with distinction at Durham University, and was awarded his PhD by Lancaster University. He is the author of 12 books on politics and history. As well as writing the official histories of the Amicus and GMB unions, he has edited new editions of Will Thorne's autobiography, *My Life's Battles* (Lawrence & Wishart, 2014) and Keir Hardie's *From Serfdom to Socialism* (Lawrence & Wishart, 2015).

JEREMY CORBYN, Leader of the Labour Party, has been MP for Islington North since 1983. He is Chair of the Stop the War Coalition and of Liberation, Vice Chair of the Campaign for Nuclear Disarmament and active on human rights issues in Parliament.

BOB HOLMAN is a writer and community activist. He was clerk in the Post Office and after national service he studied at London University. He was a childcare officer and then an academic before starting a community project on a council estate in Bath. Subsequently, he and wife Annette moved to do similar work in her native Glasgow where they helped start a community project, Family Action, in Rogerfield and Easterhouse. He has written several books, including *Keir Hardie: Labour's Greatest Hero*, 2010 (to be reprinted this year) and *Woodbine Willie: An Unsung Hero of World War One*, 2013.

CATHY JAMIESON is a founding member of the Keir Hardie Society, and is currently the society's President. She was born and brought up in Ayrshire, and served as MSP for Carrick, Cumnock and Doon Valley from 1999–2011 and MP for Kilmarnock and Loudoun from 2010–15. She was Deputy Leader of the Scottish Labour Party from 2000–08. She has been an active trade unionist all of her working life. She is a former trustee of the Barony A Frame Trust, and continues to take in active interest in local political and mining history and heritage in Ayrshire.

WILLIAM KNOX is currently Senior Honorary Research Fellow, University of St Andrews, where he taught for many years after completing his PhD at the University of Edinburgh. He has written widely on labour history, including, *Industrial Nation: Work, Culture and Society in Scotland 1800–Present* (1999), and *James Maxton* and *Scottish Labour Leaders, 1918–1939: A Biographical Dictionary*, and numerous contributions to books and journals. Currently, along with Professor Alan McKinlay, he is researching the life of the late Jimmy Reid, as well as completing a study of interpersonal violence in Scotland, 1700–1850.

RICHARD LEONARD is GMB Scotland's Political Officer, a former chairperson of the Scottish Labour Party, he is the longest serving member of its elected Executive. He has been the Secretary of the Keir Hardie Society since its establishment in 2010. He is also the Vice-Chairperson of the Scottish Labour History Society. In 2011 he stood for the Scottish Parliament in the Carrick, Cumnock and Doon Valley constituency. For over 20 years he has been a regular writer and campaigner on Scottish politics, the Scottish economy and the importance of working-class and labour history.

OWEN SMITH is Labour's Shadow Work and Pensions Secretary. His constituency and hometown of Pontypridd neighbours the Merthyr Boroughs represented by Keir Hardie. He was elected in 2010 and has served as a shadow minister in the Health and Treasury teams before joining the Shadow Cabinet in 2012. Prior to election, Owen worked as a BBC journalist and as a company director in the biotech industry. In 2012 he co-edited with Rachel Reeves MP, a collection of essays on 'One Nation Labour'.

DAVE WATSON is Head of Bargaining and Campaigns at UNISON Scotland. He is a past Chair of the Scottish Labour Party and current member of the Scottish Executive Committee. He is Secretary of the Scottish Labour Trade Union Committee and Secretary of the Scottish Health Association. He has contributed to books and journals and is a regular blogger at www.unisondave.blogspot.co.uk.

BARRY WINTER worked for the ILP for many years and is a member of its National Administrative Council. He taught Politics at Leeds Metropolitan University. He is currently rewriting a pamphlet on history of the ILP. He chairs Northern Futures at the Hannah Mitchell Foundation and is on the committee of Leeds Taking Soundings and Leeds for Change.

Viewpoints is an occasional series exploring issues of current and future relevance.
Luath Press is an independently owned and managed book publishing company based in Scotland, and is not aligned to any political party or grouping.

What Would Keir Hardie Say?

Exploring Hardie's vision and relevance to 21st Century politics

Edited by PAULINE BRYAN

with contributions by

FRAN ABRAMS, MELISSA BENN, CATHY JAMIESON,
JOHN CALLOW, JEREMY CORBYN, BOB HOLMAN,
WILLIAM KNOX, RICHARD LEONARD, OWEN SMITH,
DAVE WATSON and BARRY WINTER

Ginny,
from Kahin a
November 2015

Luath Press Limited

EDINBURGH

www.luath.co.uk

First published 2015
Reprinted 2015

ISBN: 978-1-910745-15-1

The authors' right to be identified as author of this book
under the Copyright, Designs and Patents Act 1988 has been asserted.

The paper used in this book is recyclable. It is made from low chlorine pulps
produced in a low energy, low emission manner from renewable forests.

Printed and bound by Bell and Bain Ltd., Glasgow

Typeset in 11 point Sabon

© Keir Hardie Society and the contributors 2015

Contents

MAKING HIS MARK

BEFORE EVERYTHING ELSE

Chronology

1856 Keir Hardie is born on 15 August in Legbrannock, North Lanarkshire, Scotland.

1864 Hardie gains his first job working as a message boy for the Anchor Line Steamship Company.

1866 Hardie is hired as a trapper and works in the mines at Newarthill Colliery. Largely self-taught, he begins to attend night school around this time.

1879 In August Hardie assumes his first ever union role as a Miners Agent.

1880–81 The First Boer War.

1885 Allan Octavian Hume founds the Indian National Congress in Calcutta in late December.

1888 On 27 April Hardie stands for election as an MP for the first time and comes last in the Mid Lanarkshire by-election.
On 25 August Hardie and other activists form the Scottish Labour Party, with Hardie becoming the party's secretary.

1892 Hardie stands for election in West Ham South and wins. He takes his seat in Parliament for the first time on 3 August. He is ridiculed by his fellow MPs for the relative informality of his dress.

1893 Hardie founds the Independent Labour Party (ILP) in Bradford in a two-day conference in January that had been planned the previous year.

1894 251 miners die in an explosion in a colliery near Pontypridd. Hardie requests that Parliament append a note of condolence to the miners' families to a Parliamentary address on the new royal baby. When this is refused, Hardie delivers a speech in Parliament criticising the monarchy.

1895 Hardie loses his seat in the House of Commons.

1897 The National Central Society for Women's Suffrage and the National Society for Women's Suffrage unite under Millicent Fawcett to form the National Union of Women's Suffrage Societies.

1899 The Second Boer War begins.
Hardie lodges a motion at the Trade Union Congress to form a distinct labour group within Parliament; this is passed, forming the Labour Representation Committee.

1900 Heavily influenced by the Boer War in what historians refer to as the Khaki election, Lord Salisbury's Government is returned to power with a Parliamentary majority. Labour wins just two seats, one of which was Keir Hardie in Merthyr Tydfil and Aberdare.

1902 The Second Boer War ends.

1903 Emmeline Pankhurst founds the Women's Social and Political Union. This is more commonly known as the Suffragettes.

1906 The Labour Representation Committee, now with 29 seats following the 1906 election, formally adopts the name 'The Labour Party'. The Independent Labour party affiliates itself to the Labour Party, and Hardie serves as the first Leader of the Labour Party.

1907–1908
Hardie embarks on a tour of the British empire, visiting India, Australasia, and South Africa.
Hardie resigns as leader of the Labour Party.

1909 In September the British government introduces force feeding in British prisons to counteract women going on hunger strike in pursuit of suffrage.

1912 Parliament introduces Home Rule for Ireland.
1913 In April, the Cat and Mouse Act (which allows hunger striking suffrage activists to be released and then re-imprisoned after they recover) is passed.

1914 Against the protestation of Hardie, the United Kingdom enters the First World War on 4 August.

1915 Hardie dies on 26 September as a result of several strokes.

1916 From 24 to 29 April an armed uprising attempts to end British rule in Ireland and establish an Irish Republic. The incident, which becomes known as Easter Rising, is swiftly crushed by the British army.

1917 22–27 February, Russian Revolution and abdication of Tsar Nicholas II, followed by 26 October Revolution when the Bolshevik Party, led by Vladimir Lenin, takes power.

1918 In January, Scot John Maclean is elected to the chair of the Third All-Russian Congress of Soviets. The following month he is appointed Bolshevik consul in Scotland. Sylvia Pankhurst is invited to Moscow by Lenin, leader of the Russian Communist Party.
On 6 February Parliament passes the 1918 Representation of the People Act, giving women over the age of 30 the right to vote for the first time.
On 11 November Germany signs an armistice with the Entente Powers, effectively ending the First World War.
Later in November Parliament passes the Eligibility of Women Act, allowing women to be elected as MPs.

1919– 1921 The Irish War of Independence.

1922 Parliament passes the Irish Free State Constitution Act, establishing what would become the Republic of Ireland. Northern Ireland is given the option of withdrawing from the free state.

1924 Ramsay MacDonald becomes Prime Minister on 22 January, leading the first (minority) Labour government.

1928 On 2 July Parliament passes the 1928 Representation of the People Act, giving women equal voting rights with men in the UK.

1932 The ILP disaffiliates from the Labour Party.

1939 The UK enters the Second World War.

1945 On 26 July Clement Attlee becomes Prime Minister with Labour's first ever majority in the House of Commons.
Following the atomic bombings of Hiroshima and Nagasaki, Japan surrenders on 15 August, this effectively brings the Second World War to an end.

1946 Parliament passes the National Health Service Act.

1947 The British Raj is partitioned into India and Pakistan as both gain independence from the British empire.

1948 The National Health Service Act comes into effect on 5 July.

1964–70
A Labour Government is returned with a small majority. Harold Wilson becomes Prime Minister. Re-elected in 1966 with a comfortable 97 majority. Enacts legislation on equal pay, decriminalises homosexuality and abortion. The Social Contract with trade unions ends in greater industrial unrest. Conservatives win the 1970 Election.

1974 Edward Heath calls an election in response to the miners' strike, asking 'Who Governs Britain?' Labour wins two elections in the same year with only a slim majority.

1975 The ILP rejoins the Labour party as Independent Labour Publications, a left wing pressure group within the party.

1979 A Conservative Government is elected with Margaret Thatcher as its leader (the first and, so far, only female Prime Minister of the UK). The Conservatives remain in power until 1997.

1981 The Gang of Four – Roy Jenkins, David Owen, Bill Rogers and Shirley Williams – break from Labour to form the Social Democratic Party.

1995 The Labour Party revises Clause IV of its constitution to no longer advocate for the common ownership of the means of production.

1997 Labour is returned with a 179 overall majority. Tony Blair becomes Prime Minister and Gordon Brown Chancellor of the Exchequer. Labour is re-elected in 2001 and 2005. Gordon Brown becomes Leader and Prime Minister in 2007. Labour loses the Election in 2010 with the Conservatives and Liberal Democrats forming a coalition. One of the first acts of the 1997 government is to conduct a referendum on Scottish and Welsh devolution.

1999 The Scottish Parliament, dissolved since the act of Union in 1707, reconvenes on 12 May.

2010 On 15 August the Keir Hardie Society is founded at the Summerlee Museum of Scottish Industrial Life.

Acknowledgements

I would like to thank the authors for their contributions which, when brought together, give us a rounded view of a complex individual. Far from being a mythical figure from history, they make Keir Hardie's life into a totally relevant touchstone for the present day. A special word of thanks to Jennie Renton of Luath Press for her attention to detail and enthusiasm for the book.

I would also like to thank Dolores May Arias, Hardie's great-granddaughter, whose Foreword warmly acknowledges how her mother passed on to her a sense of his values. Her own daughter came with her to Cumnock a few years ago to keep that family link alive. Hardie had a special affinity with children and would always be ready to fight for their future so that they could 'live for the better day'.

Pauline Bryan

Foreword

WHEN I WAS first asked to write a Foreword for this book about my great-grandfather's legacy, a panic ensued. Although I always had a general understanding of his role in British labour history, I felt ill-prepared to contribute any profound insights into his life and work. Most of my knowledge of Keir Hardie and his place in Scottish history was based on limited readings and rather vague family stories. But in some ways, he always has been a part of my life as well, and I think it is hard to capture this without recognising my mother, Jean Hardie Scott, as the link. It was she that imparted pride in her grandfather, and felt the importance of passing along his values through her own words and actions.

As my mother would often admit when asked about her memories of her grandfather, she actually had none of her own, as she was born in December 1916, over a year after his death. What she did know was that, while some people in the family's home town of Cumnock in Ayrshire did not agree with his politics, they admired and respected him as a gentleman.

It may seem strange that Keir Hardie's only direct descendants are Americans, but my grandfather moved to the US as a young man and settled here, never again returning to Scotland. He married his childhood sweetheart, May Stoddart, a Cumnock girl, in 1912. She was escorted to the US on a ship by her soon to be father-in-law, Keir Hardie. They wed in Brooklyn, NY. Although their only child, Jean, was born in the United States, Scotland was always in her blood and close to her heart. While my grandfather became a US citizen and never returned to Scotland, my grandmother travelled home frequently. My mother often accompanied her. I have a photo of her as a toddler in the gardens of *Lochnorris* with her grandmother, Lillie Hardie.

At the age of 12, my mother was sent to live with her Stoddart aunts in Cumnock and eventually attended nursing school at the Glasgow Royal Infirmary, graduating in 1940 with her RN and the bronze medal. Her training took her to London during the Blitz, and when the war was almost over, she returned to her parents' home in Hartford, Connecticut. It is there she met and married my dad, Jorge Lizaso Scott, who was from Cuba and doing his medical residency at the hospital where she was working. I am their only child.

I guess at some level I always knew that my great-grandfather was a special person. Most likely seeing the bust in front of the town hall in Cumnock helped me with this realisation. Of course, each visit to Cumnock had to include a family photo in front of the statue. Then in college I took a British History class, and when the instructor actually knew about Keir Hardie, it was a 'wow' moment. So of course, I did some further research, and that was my first introduction to his politics.

Visits to *Lochnorris*, Keir Hardie's home in Cumnock, were always fun for me as a child. Uncle Emrys* and his second wife, Aunt Mattie, made it their home. He made sure I knew how important my great-grandfather had been.

In 1992 my mother and I were invited to attend a variety of events celebrating the 1892 election of Keir Hardie to Parliament. In London we were invited to a tea at the Houses of Parliament hosted by Tony Benn MP, saw a showing of the play *A Better Day* and visited a special commemorative exhibit at a local museum. Cumnock also showed its pride by organising a weekend full of events, including dedication of plaques along Keir Hardie Trail, a luncheon at the Royal Hotel, an evening dance, a lively block (street) party on Keir Hardie Hill and a Sunday church service at Keir Hardie's place of worship.

When I look back upon my mother's life and what she valued and strived for, I understand the influence that the Hardie legacy had on her. She was a kind, loyal person who always fought for the underdog, and was not shy about letting her feelings be known when she felt there was an injustice that needed to be corrected. To be honest, my father and I would frequently cringe when she was making her points in public, but she was always the advocate and never shrunk from speaking her mind. I definitely can see that she carried on the Hardie family tradition with integrity. She returned to Scotland to visit many times, but in 1998, shortly after my father died, she asked my family to accompany her to Scotland for her final visit.

Near the end of her days, she often begged me to take her home and I promised that I would try to get her back to her own house for a short stay... it was only a couple of miles away. It was heartbreaking when I realised that when she said she wanted to go 'home', she really meant she wanted to go back to Cumnock.

Dolores May Arias, Rhode Island, USA

---

*Emrys Hughes was Member of Parliament for South Ayrshire 1946–69. His family were long-term friends of Keir and Lillie Hardie and in 1924 he married their daughter Nan.

Introduction

KEIR HARDIE ENTERED Parliament on 3 August 1892 dressed as a working man, a working man in his Sunday best, but clearly and identifiably, a working man. He walked by the vaulted arches, the elaborately engraved ceilings, the murals, the marble floors, the livery wearing messengers and his fellow MPs wearing top hats and morning dress. He wore a cloth cap, checked trousers and a red scarf. He said later in an interview, 'I had always worn a tweed cap and homespun clothes and it never entered my head to make a change.'[1]

This wasn't a faux pas but a deliberate decision about what sort of public representative he was going to be. Some two decades later James Maxton said, in his own maiden speech in Parliament:

> We admit frankly that perhaps on the nicer points of good form we have different ideas from Hon members on the other side of the House. Our dialect is somewhat different also, and perhaps our mode of dressing is slightly different. But we think it is the very worst form, the very worst taste, that is shows very bad breeding, to kick a man who is in the gutter, or to withdraw a crust from a starving child.[2]

Hardie was often booed and laughed at by his fellow MPs, but he exposed them time and again for their lack of compassion and obsequiousness. But as Dolores May Arias says in her Foreword, where it mattered, such as at home in Cumnock, he was admired and respected as a gentleman.

When Hardie died 14 months into the First World War one of the many moving obituaries came from Scottish-born Irish Republican James Connolly. They had disagreed on many occasions, but Connolly wrote:

> By the death of Comrade James Keir Hardie labour has lost one of its most fearless and incorruptible champions, and the world one of its highest minded and purest souls.
>
> It is not easy for us who knew him long and personally to convey to the reader how much of a loss his taking away is to the labour movement. We feel it with the keenness of a personal loss.
>
> James Keir Hardie was to the labour movement a prophetic anticipation of its own possibilities. He was a worker, with all

the limitations from which no worker ever completely escapes, and with potentialities and achievements such as few workers aspire after, but of which each worker may be the embodiment.[3]

Connolly's comment that Hardie 'was to the labour movement a prophetic anticipation of its own possibilities' is reflected throughout this book, as each author explores aspects of his full and varied life. The British Labour Party was largely his creation and it did, in its early years embody his spirit.

In his biography, Kenneth O Morgan details the continuing influence of Hardie in the first 30 years of the party; its hatred of unemployment, its support for the League of Nations and colonial liberation and the continuing central role of the trade unions. He identifies 1931 onwards as the period when the party began to 'emerge from the era of Keir Hardie'.[4]

The party changed within 30 years, from its early leaders who had little formal education, who had worked in manual jobs but were often great orators, to a very different manner of leader. He cites Hugh Dalton and a group of young economists associated with him, which included Hugh Gaitskell, Anthony Crosland and Roy Jenkins, who set out to transform the Labour Party. While Harold Wilson might have said in his 1961 Labour Party Conference speech *The Labour Party is a moral crusade or it is nothing*' these early day modernisers set out to change it from a party of socialism to one of pragmatism. This eventually left it vulnerable to the likes of Tony Blair to adopt clearly neo-liberal policies.

Before 1935, the party had seven leaders who had been a miner, a foundry man, a shipyard worker, a farm labourer, a miner, a mill worker and a manual labourer respectively. After 1935, all but two were Oxbridge or ancient Scottish university educated with very different careers from their early counterparts. It could be argued that when the Labour Party ceased to be the party of Keir Hardie it began to lose the support of working people.

Part of the reason for that loss of support was that it also ceased its role in shaping working people's understanding of the world from a class perspective and simply presented it through the same prism as the Conservatives and Liberals. All that was left for it was to introduce some minor modifications to the system, but never to change it. Harold Laski, when he was Labour Party Chairman in 1945, claimed that Hardie had provided the 'two essential keys to the party's progress. He had stressed the belief in the solidarity of the working class. And he had urged that Labour's programme must be based firmly on ethical foundations.'[5]

The aim of this book is to highlight aspects of Hardie's life and work and to draw from them relevance to the present day.

Guiding Principles

In the opening section on Hardie's guiding principles, Richard Leonard tackles Hardie's socialism. Hardie is often dismissed as having no real theoretical underpinning to his socialism. It is clear that his life was spent mostly in action. He certainly never saw his role as constructing a vast critical analysis in the style of Marx, but neither was he a pragmatist like the other MPs elected alongside him in 1892 who entered Parliament on an independent labour ticket and promptly joined the Liberal benches. He wrote copiously, from writing a regular column in a local paper from his mid-20s, to editing *The Miner*, the *Labour Leader*, producing numerous pamphlets and, of course, innumerable speeches. Richard argues that he presented an understanding of socialism that was accessible to working people and through that helped build a movement.

Bob Holman writes of Hardie's Christianity. He was evangelical in his politics, his temperance and his Christianity. He was, however, far from a conventional Victorian Christian. While he may have looked like an Old Testament Prophet, it was as Bob says, the image of Christ being close to the poor that he most identified with. He had many conflicts with more conservative Christians who promised a better after life, most famously with Lord Overtoun who simultaneously forced his employees to work in unbearable conditions on Sunday and campaigned against the running of trams on the Sabbath. Hardie would always expose the hypocrisy of the supposedly Christian ruling class.

The third guiding principle of Hardie's political life was internationalism. And from that he developed his opposition to colonialism and war. Jeremy Corbyn MP, who could be said to embody much of the spirit of Keir Hardie in the House of Commons today, writes of his lasting contribution in turning the British labour movement outwards to look at the struggles of working people in other lands. Hardie was an early opponent of Britain's vast appetite for colonies and he supported Indian independence at a time when to most it was inconceivable. He went on to take the most unpopular position of his political life, to campaign against the First World War. No matter the personal cost, he could not do otherwise. In a speech in Parliament at the outbreak of war in 1914, he said, 'A few years hence... we shall look back in wonder and amazement at the flimsy reasons which induced the Government to take part in it.'[6]

Causes and Campaigns

All through his life Hardie was a campaigner. Reading about his life at a time when travel and communication took so much time and effort, he appears to have gone everywhere. He endlessly crisscrossed the country and the world in support of campaigns and strikes.

It was, of course, the trade union movement that brought him into politics. William Knox describes Hardie's most central contribution to the British labour movement, the bringing together of socialist parties and groups together with the trade union movement in order to form a Labour Party. As James Connolly said of Hardie:

> Hence I have come to the belief that Keir Hardie was wise in his generation when he worked to form the Labour Representation Committee and that he showed a nearer approximation to the spirit of the much quoted phrase of Marx about the Trade Unions alone being able to form the political party of Labour, than any of our revolutionaries... ever did or do.[7]

During the years in which he campaigned to establish a party of the labour movement, he helped establish, first the Scottish Labour Party, then the Britain-wide Independent Labour Party and eventually the Labour Party as a federation of political groups and trade unions. As Barry Winter points out, the strained relationship between the ILP and the Labour Party prefigured the challenge faced by many on the left within the Labour Party. It was the ILP, however, that remained closest to Keir Hardie's heart.

It is perhaps his support for the Women's Suffrage movement, and most particularly the Pankhursts' Women's Social and Political Union, that most troubled many of Hardie's friends and comrades. Fran Abrams explores why it was so central to him, and why he rejected the alternative campaign supported by most women members of the ILP. There were, of course, many in the labour movement who condemned him for supporting women's suffrage under any circumstances. In other ways Hardie was a man of his time, but on this issue, as Fran says, he was ahead of his time.

Dave Watson unpicks an issue of immense interest to the present day: was Keir Hardie a nationalist? We know for certain that he supported Home Rule for Ireland, Scotland and Wales. It was, however, not on the basis of nationalist aspirations, but rather to achieve a decentralisation of democracy. He was strongly committed to local democracy in both political and trade union institutions, but also wanted there to be British and Irish solidarity when it came to fighting for working people.

Making His Mark

It was a long journey from being a young trade union representative in Cumnock, in Ayrshire, to becoming the Leader of the British Labour Party, travelling Europe, Africa, Asia and America to campaign for an international movement of socialists. Cathy Jamieson describes the impact that Keir Hardie had in Ayrshire, and how he continues to be a touchstone for judging whether the Labour Party is living up to his standards. While he was away from home for most of his time, he claimed to have kept his watch set at Cumnock time:

> By keeping to Cumnock time I could always tell exactly what was being done at home, when the children went to school, when they returned, when they went to bed.[8]

His upbringing and early experiences kept him rooted and at ease with working people everywhere.

His first time in Parliament as an MP for West Ham South was not a happy experience. He described the House of Commons 'as a place which I remember with a haunting horror'. This was no reflection on West Ham which was, as described by John Callow, 'a good fit' for Hardie. Local voters had become radicalised through the work of trade union leaders such as Will Thorne and when the opportunity presented itself to have an independent labour candidate they chose Hardie. Three years later, however, for various reasons his support had fragmented and the moment passed. A Tory was returned with a much lower turnout by the electors. Hardie learned an important lesson that what was needed was an organised Party, not individual independent MPs.

Hardie's next experience in Parliament came as the MP for Merthyr Tydfil in South Wales. Owen Smith, MP for Pontypridd which neighbours the Merthyr Boroughs, says that Merthyr and Hardie was a match made in heaven. As in West Ham, there was a radicalised electorate: the people of Merthyr kept true to the memory of Henry Richard, who had represented the area until 1888 and who had been an advocate of Peace. Hardie's opposition to the Boer War, in many places unpopular, here found a receptive audience. Merthyr was his second home, after Cumnock, and he formed close and lasting relationships, not least with the family of his future son-in-law, Emrys Hughes.

The Agitator

The final essay comes from Melissa Benn, Hon President of the Keir Hardie Society. She puts her finger on the essence of the man. He was, as described by his first biographer and friend William Stewart, 'before everything else, an agitator'. This had at times bought him adulation, but when he adopted unpopular campaigns, such as to stop the war in 1914, he was vilified in the press and in the street. Melissa believes that a Hardie of today would still be agitating, would still be supporting campaigns that challenge mainstream thinking, and would still be risking the avalanche of abuse from the media and would still have a strong influence within the movement and the country.

At the time of writing, one of the authors, Jeremy Corbyn, is a candidate for the leadership of the Labour Party. He is receiving huge levels of support and speaking to large crowds wherever he goes. He is reaching out beyond the existing membership of the Labour Party and trade unions and reawakening a sense of excitement about politics. Whatever the eventual outcome, this leadership election will leave a legacy of a type of politics that is closer to that promoted by Keir Hardie than we have seen for generations.

At the time of reprinting, one of the authors, Jeremy Corbyn, has just been elected Leader of the Labour Party. He is receiving huge levels of support and speaking to large crowds wherever he goes. He is reaching out beyond the existing membership of the Labour Party and trade unions and reawakening a sense of excitement about politics. The leadership election has already changed the Labour Party. Hundreds of thousands of new members and joined or rejoined. The impact will leave a legacy of a type of politics that is closer to that promoted by Keir Hardie than we have seen for generations.

Pauline Bryan
Glasgow, September 2015

'Socialism implies the inherent equality of all human beings.'

CHAPTER I

Socialism: More than a Creed

Richard Leonard

THROUGHOUT HIS LIFE, James Keir Hardie remained a visionary dedicated to the creation of a socialist society and the means for achieving it would, he believed, be an independent working class party based on the trade unions, the Labour Party.

To commemorate Keir Hardie is not to look wistfully backwards but to remind ourselves of the absolute necessity of unflinching principles, vision and determination in looking forward.

Hardie believed that the truths about socialism were self-evident and his conception of it was rooted in ethical values and moral courage. This led contemporaries like J Bruce Glasier to claim that Hardie's socialism was neither 'scientific nor Utopian',[1] insisting that he had no time for Marx or any socialist theory.

He was guided by religious, or perhaps I should say, moral convictions, rather than by philosophical theorising or scientific analyses of economic or social phenomena.[2]

And so for many years this was the received view of Hardie's socialism: moderate, free of dogma, romantic, moral in force, and whilst it is most of these it cannot be limited to each of these.

This view of Hardie as the moderate socialist has often been supported by the citation of a two part article Hardie wrote for the *Labour Leader* in 1904 entitled 'An Indictment of the Class War' in which he declared that 'Socialism makes war upon a system, not upon a class...'[3]

Yet Hardie clearly understood the class-based nature of the capitalist society he lived in and consequently had no hesitation in appealing to workers as a class. He sought not to modestly tinker with the structure of society but rather to radically change it from the root up. His ultimate aim was to create the necessary and sufficient conditions for the abolition of capitalism and its replacement with a new society, a classless, socialist commonwealth.

He understood, too, that the agency for change was a unified and organised working class, whose role was not simply to intervene in the labour market to mitigate some of the economic system's wilder excesses, but to act as a social force to challenge the very principle and existence of that system.

And so in *From Socialism to Serfdom*, the fullest statement of Hardie's socialist gospel, described in his own humble words as 'a brief unadorned statement of the case for Socialism, easily understandable by plain folk...'[4] Whilst he unashamedly appeals to the middle class, he declares that

> it is to the working class itself that we must look for changing the system of production and making it a means of providing for the healthy human need of all the people. This is so not only because of their numbers but also because unless they consciously set themselves to win Socialism it can never be won.[5]

The decisive struggle for Hardie and the very essence of socialism itself was a redistribution of not just wealth, but power, from those who own the wealth to those who through their hard work and endeavour create it. His language was that of emancipation, the long march of humanity to economic, social, political and international emancipation.

In Hardie's view, that liberation struggle and that emancipation were not a historical inevitability, nor a force of nature, but would be brought about by organisation, education and agitation. It demanded reasoned persuasion that it was realisable, as well as inspirational leadership and powerful ideas to drive forward a great social movement.

Taking a Class View

Whilst Glasier is right to claim that Hardie eschewed arid dogma and rigid theory, his analysis is very close to that of Marx and Engels in investing his faith in the rising confidence of the organised working class as the agent for transformative change. Moreover at a rather basic level his socialist economics echo those of Karl Marx who in Volume III of *Das Kapital* identifies 'three great classes' in society: the owners of labour power (wage-labourers); the owners of capital (profit-takers); and the owners of land (rent-receivers).

So in *From Serfdom to Socialism,* Hardie makes clear that

> the economic object of Socialism, therefore is to make land and industrial capital common property, and to cease to produce for the profit of the landlord and the capitalist and to begin to produce for the use of community.

In the bibliography at the end of the book he offers 'A Selection of Writings for the guidance of those who desire to learn more about Socialism and the Modern Labour Movement.' The very first book recommended is *Capital* by Karl Marx.

We also know from Hardie's book collection, magnificently curated and on permanent display at the Baird Institute in Cumnock, Ayrshire, that he did hold in his personal library an 1891, fourth edition of *Capital* translated from the German edition by Samuel Moore and Edward Aveling and edited by Frederick Engels. From the same source we also know that he had a copy of the first English language biography of Marx, *Karl Marx: His Life and Work,* published in New York by BW Huebsch. The book bears an inscription from its author: 'To Jas Keir Hardie, with the affectionate regards from his old comrade-in-arms. John Spargo, May 1910'.

Jimmy Maxton later wrote of Hardie that whatever his view of Marxist theory 'in practice his own activities show he was probably more Marxist than those who paid deference to Marxist theories.'[6] And in his pamphlet *My Confession of Faith in the Labour Alliance* written in 1909 as a passionate rejoinder to attacks on the Labour Party by Victor Grayson, Robert Blatchford and Henry Hyndman Hardie drew on Marx and Engels extensively to describe the Labour Party as 'the only expression of orthodox Marxian Socialism in Great Britain' and the Labour Party's founders 'in the direct line of apostolic succession from Marx and the other great masters of Socialist theory and policy.'[7] Albeit that this is probably designed more out of frustration leading to provocation than fact leading to proof. All of which is not to claim Hardie as a Marxist, but to draw due attention to the primary role which ownership, property and profit played in his understanding of how change will come to secure working-class emancipation. So it is a class struggle if not a class war which he demanded to transform society.

Harold Laski claimed that the intellectual strands of British Socialism in its pioneering phase were made up of 'Chartist radicalism, Owenite optimism, Christian Socialism, William Morris romanticism, Fabianism and Marxist materialism.'[8] Hardie's socialism borrows from a range of these intellectual traditions. Raymond Williams defines socialism as a belief that:

> Real freedom could not be achieved, basic inequalities could not be ended, social justice could not be established, unless a society based on private property was replaced by one based on social ownership and control.'[9]

This encapsulates Keir Hardie's socialism perfectly.

The *Kilmarnock Herald* of Friday January 1 1892 carries in it a report of a meeting in Port Glasgow at which Hardie as the Honorary Secretary of the Scottish Labour Party attacks a recent speech by the then Kilmarnock Burghs MP, Stephen Williamson:

> What Socialism would do was to see that the needs of the very poorest in the community were of more concern than the hoardings of the rich, and so long as there were poor people, there should not be accumulation of wealth which could not be used by the individuals in whose possession it was. Socialists did not propose to abolish capital. The Socialist did not propose to do without capital, but they wanted to abolish the capitalist who managed to live an idle life because he had a monopoly of the capital. (Applause). They proposed to nationalise capital in the same way in which they proposed to nationalise the land. [It was a] Socialism aimed at making land and capital the hand maidens not the oppressors of labour (Applause).[10]

Common Ownership

At the 1894 TUC in Norwich, Hardie successfully moved an amendment to a call to 'nationalise the land, mines, minerals and royalty rents' by seeking the deletion of the last three items enumerated and the insertion of the words 'and the whole of the means of production, distribution and exchange. In so doing, he argued that:

If the mines from which the minerals were taken were to be nationalised, why not the railways which conveyed those minerals, the depots where they were deposited, and the works in which they were manufactured... There was no reason why the landlord should be attacked and the capitalist allowed to go free.

Instead, there should be 'a genuine co-operative communal brotherhood'.[11]

Hardie's socialism is defined by the need to transform the ownership of the economic system as well as the ethics of society. But it is a call for the common ownership of the means of production, not explicitly under the control of the state (as is suggested in his later speech to Parliament in 1901), but in a free, co-operative commonwealth, which is so striking. So his vision is not to nibble away at the economic and social system but to fundamentally change it. It goes further, too, than his manifesto at the Mid Lanark by Election of 1888, in which, ironically, he called for the same demands as the TUC proposal he successfully amended six years later. That is, the establishment of a Ministry of Mines and the nationalisation of royalties and minerals.

Success in a Private Members' Ballot ensured that the first motion on socialism ever tabled in the House of Commons was debated on 23 April 1901. Hardie, by then the Member of Parliament for Merthyr Tydfil, spoke of mass poverty and misery on the one hand and the accumulation of wealth in the hands of a few on the other. But the case he makes is also for a socialism with a discernible William Morris influence. There are comparisons to the pre-industrial revolution age of 'no machinery, no large capitalists, no private property in land', a bygone era of 'more happiness, more comfort and more independence'. Significantly, Hardie believed Morris to be 'the greatest man whom the Socialist movement has yet claimed in this country...'[12]

In the parliamentary debate, Hardie declared the choice for the nation to be

between an uncontrolled monopoly conducted for the benefit and in the interests of its principal shareholders, and a monopoly owned, controlled and manipulated by the state in the interests of the nation as a whole.

Socialism, by placing land and the instruments of production in the hands of the community, eliminates only the idle, useless class at both ends of the scale... Half a million of the people of this country benefit by the present system; the remaining millions of toilers and business men do not. The pursuit of wealth corrupts the manhood of men. We are called upon at the beginning of the 20th century to decide the question propounded in the Sermon on the Mount as to whether we will worship God or Mammon. The present day is a Mammon-worshipping age. Socialism proposes to dethrone the brute-god Mammon and to lift humanity into its place.

...just as sure as Radicalism democratised the system of government politically in the last century, so will Socialism democratise the country industrially during the century upon which we have just entered.[13]

And so he called in his resolution for 'a Socialist Commonwealth founded upon the common ownership of land and capital, production for use and not for profit, and equality of opportunity for every citizen.'[14]

Hardie's Socialism is a creed with a larger transformative purpose, underpinned by a living faith in a new society founded on the concept of community rather than material wealth. But at its root it is a socialism which is economic and industrial, concerned with the ownership of the means of production, including the land. According to Hardie a socialist society begins to be realised when political democracy delivers economic democracy, so that an economic as well a political system of the people, by the people, for the people is created. And with biblical reference point, it is a socialism which is ethical and Christian in outlook, yet humanitarian in its intent.

And that purposefulness is important. In *From Serfdom to Socialism*, he goes on to argue that

this change in ownership... and in the object of production, however, is merely the medium through which it is hoped the Socialist spirit will find expression. Socialism implies the inherent equality of all human beings. It does not assume that all are alike, but only that all are equal. Holding this to be true of individuals, the Socialist applies it also to races.

Taking up the theme of 'the object of production', Hardie poses the question: 'If the State can build battleships and make swords, why not also trading ships and ploughshares?'[15]

So Hardie's socialist vision is one of socially useful production, under common ownership, in a society which is demilitarised and with very different production priorities. Indeed Hardie wrote that one of the two leading points of principle for socialism was 'hostility to Militarism in all its forms and to war as a method of settling disputes between nations'.[16] The second point of principle was public ownership.

It is not only an economically grounded ethical socialism, but a democratic socialism, too. For Hardie, the cornerstone of democratic socialism is democracy and he wanted to extend the boundaries of democracy to enfranchise women in the realm of politics and to all working people in the realm of the economy.

So long as property, using the term to mean land and capital, is in the hands of a small class, the rest of the people are necessarily dependent on that class. A democracy, therefore, has no option but to seek to transform these forms of property, together with the power inherent in them, from private to public possession.[17]

Democracy Against Oppression

So is it state socialism or some other form of democratic and accountable form of common ownership which Hardie advocates? In truth, he sees more of a mosaic than a monolith.

Chapter Two of *From Serfdom to Socialism* is titled 'Municipal Socialism' and Hardie sees municipalities as pioneers of the socialist spirit. It is this spirit which was the driving force behind John Wheatley in the First Labour Government with the 1924 Housing Act. Like Hardie, Wheatley understood that there was a municipal as well as a parliamentary road to socialism. In his formative proposals for workman's cottages funded by the surpluses of the Glasgow Corporation Tramway Department Wheatley caught a glimpse of the possibilities for a national council housing programme at affordable rents which he could later bring to fruition.

Hardie also suggests that a combination of both state socialism and the co-operative movement are likely:

> To dogmatise about the form which the Socialist State shall take is to play the fool. That is a matter with which we have nothing whatever to do. It belongs to the future, and is a matter which posterity alone can decide. The most we can hope to do is to

make the coming of Socialism possible in the full assurance that it will shape itself right when it does come.[18]

Hardie's socialism had resolved its end goal, but had room for experimentation, variety and diversity in its precise organisation, not least because it would be a long revolution.

As John Wheatley later recalled, the historic mission of the Independent Labour Party was crystal clear. In Keir Hardie's own words, in the year following its foundation:

> It is perfectly evident that some new and strong force is necessary to unite the democracy against oppression, against privilege, against monopoly; and there is no force so powerful for this purpose as the force of Socialism which promises to bring about economically the same freedom we are supposed to enjoy politically and religiously. I believe the ILP has a great opportunity if, only discarding all minor issues, it remembers it is created for the purpose of realising Socialism – that that is the one item of its programme, and that the means by which it is proposed to realise Socialism is the creation of an Independent Labour Party in the House of Commons and in every representative institution.[19]

Hardie wrote in a letter to his son James in 1913 that the Labour Party was a labour alliance of socialists and trade unionists rather than 'a clear-cut, class-conscious, revolutionary Marxian, and above reproach Party...'[20]

So whilst Hardie advocated the view 'With the enfranchisement of the masses it is recognised that the ballot is much more effective than the barricade',[21] his socialism was not restricted to the parliamentary road, not merely to be legislated for but realised by the political involvement of socialists 'in every representative institution' from the School Board to the Municipal Chamber, from the trade union to the co-operative society, from the Friendly Society to the Labour Party itself. But in all cases it was not enough to merely administer the state better than the Conservatives or the Liberals but axiomatic to stand for a radically different form of society.

He called for the moral and material elevation of the poor, but a redistribution of power, too: 'a people depressed, weakened, and enervated by poverty and toil are more likely to sink into a nation of spiritless serfs than to rise in revolt against their lot...'[22]

We live in a country where a small elite still own most of the land, where capital accumulation and the profit motive still dominate the legal framework of business and consequently there is little scrutiny or accountability of corporate decision makers who wield enormous power and yet are beyond the reach of our democracy. So there has been a faltering in the belief that socialist change is possible and even if it is, that the party which Keir Hardie and the trade unions founded is the vehicle to achieve it. And yet since Hardie's time we have seen Labour Governments elected and delivering progressive change from the 1924 Housing Act to the 1998 Scotland Act. Over decades, this has included the post-war attack on poverty with the development of the welfare state and establishment of the NHS, the 1945 generation's commitment to public ownership using nationalisation, the abolition of the death penalty in the 1960s, and the health and safety and equalities legislation of the 1970s. Attempts at extending industrial democracy, enacting land reform in Scotland, in growing industrial common ownership have all been initiated by Labour Governments, including those in the devolved Scottish Parliament.

Socialist Renewal

Hardie's inspiring vision of socialism still offers a convincing alternative to the present dismal social and economic order. Poverty in the midst of plenty would in Hardie's view pose a moral as well as an economic and social challenge. But he would still find its answer in that fundamental change in property relations he understood to be necessary.

The most recent crisis in the capitalist financial system should have brought into sharper focus that distinction of Hardie's between the wage-labourers, the owners of capital and the landlord class. Instead it has been blurred by the false trail of nationalism and poisoned by the bitter fruit of divide and rule which has allowed those who still own and run the economy to carry on unimpaired.

In 1907 Hardie wrote a postcard to Andrew Fisher, the Labour Prime Minister of Australia and a former Ayrshire miner, containing a simple message: 'Fraternal Greetings from the workers in the Old Home Land to their comrades in the new. The aim of our world wide movement is the same – the Economic Emancipation of earth's toiling millions.'[23] The short greeting made it clear that Labour was internationalist, and part of a great social movement not merely a protest movement, with a goal of liberation which was political in effect, economic in cause, and worldwide in scope.

As Francis Johnson writes, 'As a Socialist Internationalist, Keir Hardie held socialism transcended Nationalism.'[24] Hardie nailed his colours to an internationalist cosmopolitan mast:

> Workers are uniting under the crimson banner of a world embracing principle which knows nor sect, nor creed, nor race and which offers new life and hope to all created beings – the glorious Gospel of Socialism.[25]

Now more than ever we need socialist renewal in this spirit, offering the prospect of equality, extended democracy and social cohesion, building the co-operative socialist commonwealth which Hardie spoke so much about – not just mounting a case against capitalism or even for its reform, but putting forward the positive case for the socialist alternative. We need those enduring moral values and that understanding of history if we are to shape the future.

In that sense, the Labour Party needs to be revivalist: reviving faith, trust and confidence to meet the hopes of the people, addressing anew the very things it was brought into existence to change. For the challenges we face are not the occasion for retreat, but for defiance and advance.

At a point when, not least in the country of his birth, the whole purpose of the party Hardie created is being brought into question, the timeless appeal and the enduring message of hope in the final passage of *From Serfdom to Socialism* is worth recalling:

> Socialism with its promise of freedom, its larger hope for humanity, its triumph of peace over war, its binding of the races of the earth into one all-embracing brotherhood, must prevail.[26]

'Any system of production or exchange
which sanctions the exploitation
of the weak by the strong or the
unscrupulous is wrong and therefore
sinful.'

CHAPTER 2

Christianity: Christian and Socialist

Bob Holman

FEW VICTORIANS COULD have had childhoods which actually discouraged Christianity. Keir Hardie did. His mother Mary and stepfather David abandoned religion under the influence of the free thinker Charles Bradlaugh, although it is not known how they came under his teachings. Keir was not sent to Sunday School or church and the bible was not read to him.

He recounts an incident which took place when he was about ten which had a profound effect on him. His stepfather was away seeking work, one of his brothers was confined to the room in which they all lived and his mother was heavily pregnant. Hardie was the sole earner, doing over 12 hours a day for 3/6d a week. Up in the night looking after his brother and mother, he was twice late for work, and was summoned to explain himself to the rich baker for whom he did deliveries. After waiting while the master conducted family prayers, he was ushered into a room where a lavish breakfast was being served, to be rebuked, sacked and fined his week's money. He returned to a cold home which contained not a crust of bread and where a baby was soon to be born. Years later Hardie wrote, 'the memory of those early days abides with me, and makes me doubt the sincerity of those who make pretence in their prayers'.[1]

However, his mother and stepfather were not adverse to Keir receiving school lessons from Dan Craig, an evangelical minister from Hamilton. David Hardie could be a heavy drinker and Mary encouraged Keir to join the local branch of a temperance society called the Good Templars even though it had close links with churches. He took the pledge when he was 17 and kept to it all his life. Here he met a number of evangelical Christians who probably befriended him. It was not just

37

their religion that influenced him. The Templars lobbied local and central government to control the sale of alcohol, so his political horizons were widened. Further, it provided social activities, choirs and dances. In his late teens and early 20s, Hardie attracted the attention of several women. One was Lillie Wilson (oddly enough, the daughter of a publican), who was to become his wife.

Conversion and Church

In a scrap of a diary, Keir Hardie penned, 'Brought up an atheist – converted to Christianity in 1878.' How and why did this come about at the age of 26? Donald Carswell in *Brother Scots*, published in 1928, indicates that he was converted at a Dwight Moody mission.[2] But the Moody missions were in 1874 and 1882. The truth is not known. There is, however, a church record indicating that Keir and Lillie Hardie joined Cumnock Congregational Church on 19 July 1882.

Three of Hardie's main biographers, William Stewart,[3] Iain McLean[4] and Kenneth Morgan[5] say little about his church activities, while Margaret Cole[6] says nothing at all. It was the Minister of the Congregational Church who recommended Hardie for the post with the local paper. The Hardies were regular in attendance and Hardie sometimes preached in other churches and even in the open air, and continuing to be an enthusiastic supporter of the local temperance body. He also co-operated closely with Adam Drummond, the church secretary, who ran a foundry and blacksmith's shop and was a keen member of the Liberal Party. In a bitterly cold winter, Hardie and Drummond pioneered job creation schemes such as clearing snow off the streets and improving the local water supply.

The Cumnock archives hold an article written in 1981 by Adam Drummond's grandson, James, telling of a dispute between Hardie and Drummond. The church had a new minister, the Reverend Andrew Scott. Drummond and some other deacons considered that he was too lenient with a member, Mr Elliot, who had been drunk. Despite his temperance views, Hardie considered that the issue called for forgiveness and he and Lillie went out of their way to show kindness to the Elliots. Later, when the deacons decided to dismiss Scott, Hardie sided with him. As a result, when their second child, Sarah, was baptised, only the Scotts and the Elliots attended with them.

The upshot was that the Hardies and a number of other members left to form an evangelical church. It was part of the Evangelical Union which Professor Smout states attracted 'miners and artisans'.[7] Hardie was one of the leaders and participated in visiting the sick and dying. The church flourished for a few years.

Hardie and Socialism

At some point, Hardie ceased to be a regular attender at one particular church. This was probably because his growing political activities meant that frequently he was away speaking at weekends. He did not cease to be a Christian and his close friend, David Lowe, recorded, 'Throughout his life, Hardie never lost his faith he preached in those days'[8] – the days in Cumnock.

Hardie's conversion to Christianity occurred several years before he embraced socialism and certainly his Christianity contributed strongly to his socialism, but there were other factors. His favourite author was probably Robert Burns, whose words he cited and sang all his life. He absorbed Burn's example of the low-born making good and his insistence on the basic equality of mankind. He rejoiced in 'A Man's a Man for a' That'. He read radical authors like John Ruskin, Henry George, John Stuart Mill and the writings of Marx. During the 1880s, in Glasgow and London, he sometimes listened to contemporary socialists. Not least, he was an intuitive reformer. Even as a child, the sight of people in poverty in the midst of luxury, or the horror of seeing a mining family evicted and marched to the workhouse, filled him with a desire for social change.

Alongside all of this, his Christianity was also fundamental to his socialism. In his days at Cumnock Congregational Church, reading the bible became part of his life and in his book, *From Serfdom to Socialism*, published in 1907, he draws heavily upon the scriptures. Pointing out that from early times the Jewish people were instructed to return land to its original owner after a period of time, he cites the prophets in support of his argument that the modern system of wealth accumulation which is rooted and grounded in land monopoly, usury, and the fleecing of the poor, finds no support in the Old Testament scriptures.[9]

Above all, he identified with the Christ who was always close to the poor, who had compassion for the outcast, who forbade the accumulation of possessions, and who treated others as his brothers and sisters. His vision of socialism gave prominence to the abolition of poverty and the promotion of greater equality.

Hardie did not claim that Christianity and socialism were one and the same. He acknowledged that many non-Christians were socialists. Nonetheless, he believed that the practice of Christianity should contribute to a socialist society. As he acknowledged, very often that did not happen.

Hardie and the Churches

Hardie, backed by trade unionists, dockers and nonconformist churches – who liked his support of temperance bodies – stood for West Ham South in the General Election of 1892. He won a sensational victory over the sitting Tory MP.

Soon he became known as 'The Member for the unemployed'. With little support from other MPs, he was busy in the Commons, yet still found time to respond to church leaders who attacked socialism. A common cry from the pulpit was that religion should keep out of politics. Hardie responded:

> I lay it down as a broad, unchallengeable Christian principle that any system of production or exchange which sanctions the exploitation of the weak by the strong or the unscrupulous is wrong and therefore sinful.[10]

In 1894 Professor Flint of Edinburgh University argued in a public lecture that socialism was basically anti-Christian, because it assumed that man's chief end on earth was a happy life rather than glorifying God, because it attached more importance to the condition of men rather than their character, and because it did injustice to their rights as individuals whose money and property could be taken from them. Hardie responded that 'a man stunted in body, dwarfed in mind and sordid in spirit' could not glorify God, insisting that socialism created the better conditions which enabled characters to improve and that the rights of individuals to retain riches deprived others of the right to escape poverty. He comments, 'The more a man knows about theology, the less he is likely to know about Christianity.'[11]

A few years later he wrote scathingly about clergy who approved of the Boer War:

The politician, the financier, the business man may plead that war will benefit them... But for the minister of Christ there is no such justification. He by his office stands as the representative of Him who taught the doctrine of non-resistance...[12]

Lord Overtoun

In 1895 Hardie lost his seat in the Commons. He did not take on a well-paid position or job but devoted himself, often in poverty, to spreading socialism and publishing the *Labour Leader* in Glasgow. In 1899 he was approached by workers from Lord Overtoun's chrome factory in Rutherglen, probably the largest in the world. They showed how the chemicals had harmed their skin and lungs, and more. Hardie secretly visited the factory.

Overtoun was a Liberal lord with massive wealth. He was also a prominent Christian, a generous donor to missions and missionaries and backer of the American evangelist Dwight Moody. A strong Sabbatarian, he opposed Glasgow council's running trams on Sundays. Financially, politically, religiously, he was a giant. Hardie with little money and less power, published a pamphlet, *White Slaves*, in which he describes the factory conditions and condemns Overtoun as a Christian hypocrite, whose workers

> begin work at six in the morning. The vapours and fumes from the chemicals are about them all the time, eating away the cartilage of the nose and poisoning the blood so that the stomach in time will only contain certain types of food... a dry dust gets into the throats and produces an arid burning feeling... all the day without a break until six o'clock in the evening.

They laboured seven days a week and if they stopped on a Sunday, even to go to church, they lost a day's wages. Not that the wages were much, three or four pence an hour. No sick pay, no holiday pay, no pension. Hardie does not hide his own faith, stating his belief 'in Christ's gospel of love and brotherhood and service'.

The pamphlet was a sensation. A few Christians did support Hardie but many clergy hurled abuse at him, accusing him of being an atheist who wanted to undermine a forthcoming crusade by Moody. The printers of the pamphlet were so afraid of threats by the clergy not to employ them that they refused to print any more authored by Hardie.

Although Overtoun never responded directly, he soon made substantial increases in wages, largely abolished Sunday working and generally improved conditions for his workforce. Other factory owners did likewise. With few resources, Hardie had achieved a remarkable victory.

Gordon Brown, who studied Hardie at Edinburgh University, writes of the Overtoun affair: 'When he saw vested interests holding people back and denying them opportunity and causing them to be poor, he did not flinch from speaking out no matter the personal cost.'[13]

Christmas Embitterment

Hardie often voiced a deep disapproval of wealthy Christians who tolerated poverty. At Christmas 1897, during a strike of engineering workers, he wrote in the *Labour Leader*:

> One hundred thousand men are locked out; side by side with those are one hundred thousand women enduring bravely. At the feet of these, and looking up in mute appeal for more food are three hundred thousand children... I am afraid my heart is bitter tonight... I have known as a child what hunger means, and the scars of those days are with me still and rankle in my heart, and unfit me in many ways for doing the work waiting to be done. A holocaust of every church building in Christendom tonight would be as an act of sweet savour in the sight of Him whose name is supposed to be worshipped within their walls. If the spiritually proud and pride-blinded professors of Christianity could only be made to feel and see that the Christ is here ever present with us, and that they are laying on the stripes and binding the brow afresh with thorns and making Him shed tears of blood in a million homes, surely the world would be made more sweet for the establishment of his kingdom. We have no right to a merry Christmas which so many of our fellows cannot share.[14]

Complications

Hardie was a complicated Christian. His criticisms of church leaders have been emphasised but he also admired and joined with other leaders. Over the years, he drew the support of those known as Christian socialists like Frank Smith in London, Bream Pearce in Scotland and Fred Jowett in Bradford. When he became MP for Merthyr in Wales, he became close to the former miner and Methodist minister the Reverend John Hughes. Hughes and his wife Elizabeth backed Hardie's socialism and never wavered despite criticism from some of his congregation. Their son, Emrys, later married the Hardie's daughter Nan.

In the 1900 General Election, numbers of nonconformist churches in Merthyr were drawn to his Christian anti-war beliefs. In the election of 1910, the Anti-socialist League accused him of being an advocate of atheism and free love. Several ministers rebuked these attacks. John James, vice president of the evangelical Christian Endeavour in Wales, pleaded, 'Let us vote for Mr J Keir Hardie and practical Christianity.'[15] People did vote and Hardie was again returned with a comfortable majority.

Hardie was a straightforward, almost orthodox Christian. He did not adopt Darwinism. He did not follow the liberal theologians who cast doubts on the divinity of Christ. He regularly repeated the teachings of Christ, particularly his condemnation of riches. There was also a very real spirituality.

In 1892 after a trade union congress in Norwich, Hardie and friends strolled into the grounds of the cathedral. They watched the sun set and the darkness rise. Suddenly the voice of Hardie was heard singing the 23rd Psalm and soon the others, Christians and non-Christians, joined in. They felt at peace and at one with each other. William Stewart comments:

This inherent spiritual emotionalism – if it may be so called – was continually manifesting itself in various ways all through life, whether, as in the early Ayrshire days, in evangelising on the Ayrshire highways and byways, or, as in later days, preaching in Methodist pulpits or on Brotherhood platforms or in association with the votaries of spiritualism and theosophy. He was imbued with an imaginative catholicity of spirit which rendered him responsive to every expression of religious feeling which seemed to him sincere... It was involuntary, a part of his nature and it never hindered, but rather intensified and idealised, his work for Socialism. His spiritual enthusiasm never led him out of touch with reality. In a very literal sense, 'the poor he had always with him.' He was one of them. And to him their cause was a cause of the devotional spirit.[16]

It is difficult to explain but, from his words and from those who knew well, Hardie comes across as a man who was immune to many worldly influences. He never pursued money, status or popularity. He insisted on remaining close to working-class people even when some Labour MPs dressed and behaved like middle-class Members. Poverty and suffering moved him to tears and anger. For the sake of the poor and unemployed he was ready to take abuse, even hatred. Simultaneously, he loved nature, rivers, mountains, fields, animals. He welcomed being alone in the hills. The word 'spiritual' does aptly describe him.

Living The Life

Spirituality did not mean being vague. Hardie attempted to live out the Christian life. In a talk given in 1912 entitled 'What think ye of Christ?' he specified how Christianity should be put into practice. The following is taken from a report of the speech in a local paper.

> He would assert in the most unhesitating fashion that Christ was more concerned with establishing a kingdom upon earth than he was in thinking about a heaven in the future. In these days, the interpretation of the Gospel was mainly left to learned men, but the learned man who had not at the same time the simple mind of the peasant was incapable of understanding the Gospel of Jesus. Let them take, for example, the Sermon on the Mount. Jesus belonged to the working class, and worked at the carpenter's bench.

The reporter then adds that Hardie explained that Jesus used illustrations ordinary people could understand. The birds of the air did not worry, but they were clothed and fed. If they trusted in God, the same would happen to them. Hardie told the audience:

> He could take them to districts in London and elsewhere where mothers were sitting weeping over children who were crying in ragged clothing, boots full of holes, bellies without food... The statesmen who had the power to cure that kind of thing and did not were insulting the very name of Christ... it was up to every man and every woman who desired to see God's kingdom established on earth to do everything he or she possibly could to

overthrow an order of society based upon injustice and introduce a new order based upon fraternity and justice to all alike.[17]

The Last Years

The last years of Hardie's life saw no decline in his advocacy of socialism and his commitment to Christianity. In 1910 he was in Lille in France for a gathering of what became known as The Brotherhood, an organisation which drew in working-class members – my own father and grandfather were later to be members. Over 6,000 people crushed in to hear Hardie with many listening outside in the public square. He did not disappoint them and he included a statement he made more than once over the years: 'I myself have found in the Christianity of Christ the inspiration which first of all drove me into the movement and has carried me on in it.'[18] In 1912 he was in Wales where the Cory brothers, Christian coal owners, raised the price of coal during a bitterly cold winter. Hardie hit back, writing:

And the central fact is this: the respectable, church going men who are, without cause, raising the price of coal in the depth of winter, and raising it more against the poor, are worse than common cheats and robbers. They are robbing the poor: not merely robbing them of money but robbing them of comfort, of health and, in some cases, of life... They may attend church or chapel regularly; they may give to charities and Christian missions; they be respected members of society, patriots, and loyalists, but they are robbers all the same.[19]

On 4 August 1914 Britain declared war against Germany. Hardie opposed it. Most MPs, the press and the churches supported it. He was shouted down in his own constituency, abused in the streets, called a coward in the Commons. Numbers of friends deserted him. He was heartbroken when thousands of young, working-class men were slaughtered in the fighting. He declared, 'I understand what Christ suffered in Gethsemane as well as any man living.'[20] He refused to retreat. In October, he returned to Merthyr and was cheered. Stricken by a stroke, he carried on. He died in Glasgow of pneumonia on 26 September 1915.

He received no tributes in Parliament. No service in the Cathedral.

But his funeral cortege in Glasgow was followed by hundreds of working-class people. In church they heard about his service to Christianity and socialism. No doubt they recalled his own words, 'I am an agitator. My work has consisted of trying to stir up a divine discontent with wrong.'[21] He left little money and the Independent Labour Party paid for the funeral.

Today

Hardie died a hundred years ago. Today it is the churches which often attack politicians. Leaders from the Church of England, the Catholics and nonconformist churches condemn governments which maintain inequality and poverty. But there is no politician like Hardie who continually speaks for the poor and against government for allowing a society in which MPs are amongst the 4 per cent of top earners and whose food in the Commons is subsidised by £5m of public money, while many thousands outside turn to foodbanks.

The major parties all contain those who are acknowledged as Christians, yet few follow Hardie in arguing that poverty and inequality are unchristian. Churches and Christian MPs are reluctant to speak out against rich Christians. Tony Blair is an overt Christian who certainly does some good work, but his multi-millions and huge property portfolio serve to reinforce and sanction vast inequality. And those wealthy Christians who are large-scale tax avoiders keep money which governments could use in areas of vast deprivation.

Keir Hardie had faults and limitations which I have discussed elsewhere.[22] Yet the words of his lifelong mining friend, Bob Smilie, at a memorial service, ring true. He said:

> He was one of the most unselfish souls that ever lived. I never heard him speak of self... I never heard him express any great desire to accumulate wealth.'[23]

For me, there is something else. I look at Hardie – yes the untidy, gruff, sometimes bad-tempered Hardie – and I see his Christianity not just in his readiness to condemn the rich, but in his lifestyle and sufferings. He wanted to be near working-class people; he could weep at the sight of hungry children; he had no desire for honours or for mixing with royalty. And he accepted abuse. Early in his parliamentary career, he printed the menus from which MPs gorged themselves and contrasted the surfeit they enjoyed with the lack of choice for those who were starving. Some MPs retaliated by getting into the press stories that he was a glutton who lived in a luxurious hotel where he enjoyed champagne and ten-course meals. He received hundreds of crude and angry letters. He rarely replied to abuse. He does make me think about Christ.

'The angel of death with blood-stained wings is hovering over Europe.'

CHAPTER 3

International Peace: A Legacy for the Peace Movement

Jeremy Corbyn

ON 15 FEBRUARY 2003, well over a million people marched through London to oppose the intended invasion of Iraq. It was the biggest ever demonstration in British history. Six hundred other demonstrations took place all around the world, on every continent, including Antarctica.

They all knew why they were marching and by sheer force of numbers turned media and popular opinion around from the Government's intended story that somehow Iraq presented a threat to us all and that only by bombing could we secure the peace of the region, and indeed the world.

More than a decade later, billions spent, hundreds of thousands dead and more wars than ever, the sheer futility of war and its waste is there for all to see. The victims lie dead in unmarked graves amidst the rubble, or the soldiers from the West are in heroes' graves, in well-tended cemeteries, but still dead in their youth.

As Europe goes through a strange paroxysm of mawkish memorial of the Great War and a nasty dose of xenophobic, inward-looking behaviour, we need to learn from history of those who tried to stop that war and tried to point out where it could lead.

In my Borough of Islington, North London, we have put up a memorial plaque at the end of every street where any WWI soldiers who lost their lives once lived. It is poignant to see the names of families where all sons perished in the war and, in a close-knit community, the way in which extended families were devastated by the carnage of the Western Front.

There has also been a good discussion of the anti-war movement. In my area many of the schools have undertaken studies. I was struck by a primary school's piece of research into the life of Fenner Brockway, who was jailed and brutally treated as a conscientious objector and later went on to become a Labour MP in the forefront of the anti-imperialist movements of Britain and many other countries. His story had been put up on a tree on Highbury Fields. The children who produced this saw his life as heroic, in the same way as soldiers who died in battle were seen as heroic. This simple piece of research by bright 11-year-olds opens a whole narrative as to what is history, who is heroic and who leaves a legacy.

Around them there are other legacies, including a pub named *The Charlotte Despard*, in honour of a great suffragette, anti-war campaigner and Irish nationalist, who was also the sister of Sir John French, the first commander of the forces in Europe and later Governor General of Ireland where he brutally used the Black and Tans to suppress the thirst for liberty and independence.

Nearby is Keir Hardie House, a very well-built construction of good quality council homes and named in his honour by the council who built the estate.

Hardie's life, impressive by any standards, had a universal and global vision that was very different from many other great labour figures of the pre-1914 period. It seems astonishing, at this distance, that on 2 August 1914, two days before war was declared, he spoke in Trafalgar Square at a rally organised by the Labour Party (although initially called by the *Daily Herald*) where a declaration was adopted, which concluded by stating:

> Men and women of Britain, you now have an unexampled opportunity of showing your power, rendering magnificent service to humanity and to the world. Proclaim for you that the days of plunder and butchery have gone by. Send messages of peace and fraternity to your fellows who have less liberty than you.
>
> Down with class rule. Down with the rule of brute force. Down with the War, Up with the Peaceful Rule of the People.[1]

War, however, was declared and the Labour Party soon split between those who opposed it and those who decided to support the national endeavour of war, and later joined the coalition Government which introduced conscription and food rationing.

Hardie always opposed the war and stuck to the principles of the

Trafalgar Square manifesto. He made his position crystal clear on the day Sir Edward Grey, the Foreign Secretary, came to Parliament to announce the start of the war. Hardie was mocked by some of his fellow Labour MPs, who hummed the National anthem as he addressed the House of Commons chamber.

Eighty-nine years later, Labour Prime Minister Tony Blair told Parliament that there was no alternative to going to war with Iraq even after he and Foreign Secretary Jack Straw had failed to gain a second UN resolution specifically authorising war. Interestingly, the debate focused very much on the legality of war. While this was not something so prevalent in the opposition to WW1, Hardie did frequently invoke the Hague Conventions as a way in which the war could have been avoided.

The evening before, in the most dramatic resignation speech of all time, the late Robin Cook told Parliament why he could not support the Iraq war:

> Nothing could better demonstrate that they are wrong [commentators who claimed that Parliament was irrelevant to political decision making] than for this House to stop the commitment of troops in a war that has neither international agreement nor diplomatic support. I intend to join those tomorrow night who will vote against military action now.[2]

The legacy of Hardie, and indeed the contradictions in the Labour Party between the ideal of national war as the supreme form of patriotism, and the wider global tradition of peace and fraternity is still there and self-evidently not resolved.

Hardie and the ILP leadership continued their opposition to the war. As months, then years rolled on, jingoism and patriotism took over, and they became more isolated. Conscientious objectors suffered appalling privations in jail, or, as non-combatant stretcher bearers, died in enormous numbers.

For all the popular history of the supposed near-universal approval of WW1, it is remarkable how many of the war's opponents were elected to councils and Parliament in the 1920s.

Parallels at a century's distance are always difficult, but the millions who marched against the Iraq war in 2003 have not recanted or recoiled from the position they held; rather, many Labour MPs who supported the war lost their seats in 2005 and 2010 and in some cases issued abject apologies for their vote.

Somewhere in the midst of a century of wars and colonialism the tradition of real international solidarity has survived and now lives in a new generation in a very different world. Or looked at another way is it so different?

An International Perspective

Keir Hardie had an amazing global view; for someone who was born with no privileges of any kind, no opportunity to travel and very limited education, he had a thirst for learning and a deep appreciation of the unity of peoples in different circumstances all across the globe.

The Boer War was a turning point in British history in many ways. Provoked by the commercial interests of Cecil Rhodes and accompanied by a Whitehall assumption that it would be another minor colonial conflict, it degenerated into full-scale war, exposing the poor physique of impoverished British soldiers and the use of concentration camps by Britain. Unlike many other colonial adventures, it was not universally popular at home. Opposition was deep and widespread. It also encouraged a greater sense of international understanding, including the influential 1902 publication by JA Hobson, *Imperialism: A Study*, which was heavily influenced by the historical significance of the Boer War. Hardie not only opposed the war as being for the profits of a few, mainly Rhodes, but went on to support the Boers.

The Khaki Election of 1900 was preceded by the formation of the Labour Representation Committee and with it a rather fluid series of local organisations, mainly centred on Trades Councils. Hardie, having lost in West Ham, was looking for a new constituency. In what now seems a bizarre decision, he was adopted as a candidate for *two* constituencies, Preston and Merthyr Tydfil. A campaign spent mainly on trains between both resulted in a heavy defeat in Lancashire and a lucky win in Merthyr. Two-member constituencies were then the norm and Hardie had benefited from the perceived split in the Liberal camp, where one candidate had supported the Boer War, while the other was opposed. Hardie had support from the anti-war tradition of South Wales, especially the memory of the legendary peace MP Henry Richards, and was elected as the second member, with Liberal support. After his election victory, Hardie attributed his success to the 'uncorrupted disciples of Henry Richard'.[3] His contributions in the

Parliament until his death in 1915 show the range of his concerns, including working conditions, miners' welfare, women's suffrage and social justice. He also made an amazing variety of international journeys to the USA, India, South Africa and Australia – and numerous shorter ones in Europe, trying to build an alliance against war.

Hardie's own world view came through the prism of a vast British empire which nurtured British children in the belief that somehow they benefited from the empire and that they were superior to the rest of the world. The inherent racism in that message was powerful, and remains so. In his early days as a trade union representative he opposed Irish immigration into Scotland. Later, however, he went on to oppose segregation in South Africa during his visit there and went well beyond any other opponents of the Boer War in supporting the African and Asian peoples of South Africa.

In India he was threatened with deportation for supporting home rule and consorting with the newly formed Congress Party; his support for India's self-determination was well known and taken up in the House of Commons.

But it was his attempts to build an international peace organisation that was his most groundbreaking work. The late 19th century saw the founding of the First Working Men's International and, almost in parallel, the attempts by the Tsar of Russia and others to found an international treaty through the Hague Convention.

From the end of the Boer War onwards, as predicted in Hobson's *Imperialism*, competition between European imperialist powers intensified with flashpoints in the Balkans and also in Morocco, resulting from tension between Germany and France for pre-eminence in a nominally independent country that fell within the French sphere of influence.

Hardie managed to raise the issues of the treatment of workers in all the countries that Britain was either collaborating with (usually France), in competition with (usually Germany), or trying to form short-term alliances with (usually the Ottoman empire). His agenda was always to try and form an international peace and socialist movement and his collaboration with Jean Jaurès from France and work with the German left developed deep foundations which could have been the basis for working-class opposition to the First World War.

Hardie worked hard to unite all peace groups as though he knew the dreadful day would arrive when Britain, France, Germany, Russia and the Ottoman empire would all be at war with millions of working men lined up against each other. In the words of Kenneth Morgan's biography:

> Hardie was a central figure in every effort to superimpose the moral force of the peace movement throughout each major crisis. During the naval scare of 1908–09, when the 'dreadnoughts' programme was stepped up in response to new pressure from the German navy he spoke out powerfully against the war hysteria. He chaired a meeting at St James's Hall at which the German socialists Kautsky and Ledebour added their pleas for the call for Anglo-German amity.[4]

As war fever intensified Hardie stepped up his efforts and in 1913, only eight months before war was declared, he presided over an enormous peace rally in the Royal Albert Hall with international speakers including Jaurès. The left was not, even then, united with Hyndman of the Social Democratic federation pursuing an anti-German line.

Hardie died in 1915, essentially a broken man. All he had striven for in the sense of international working-class unity against the industrial killing machines of the Great War had been overridden by the jingoistic, crude propaganda of the allies. In all countries the labour movements split, with some joining wartime coalitions and accepting that there was a 'national' interest that was shared, however unevenly, between the aristocratic rulers and the mass of working-class people.

The Legacy

A century later, the general mood is more sanguine about the First World War. A war between nations, all led by cousins and nephews and a son of Queen Victoria, it was at once a war led by a massively dysfunctional family and the huge commercial interests that were involved.

The industrial scale of the war transformed industry and commerce across the globe: aircraft changed from being wood and string bi-planes to effective and targeted killing and observation machines; the infantry and cavalry marched behind tanks; barbed wire and mustard gas became the biggest killers of soldiers on both sides of the Western Front; submarines, first used in the American Civil War, came into their own.

At one level, it could be claimed that Britain, France and latterly the USA 'won' the war and Germany and Austria lost. The reality was, of course, far more complex, including as it did the Russian revolution and the end of its empire.

After the huge loss of life all over Europe and in the wake of the Russian revolution, in the 1920s there was a general move to the left. There was an uprising in Germany, the unrest in Scotland, in particular Red Clydeside and the growth of Communist and Socialist parties across the globe. There was also a growing anti-colonial movement across the remnants of empire. As Versailles calmly divided the world up into mandates and spheres of influence, in a manner not very different from the arrogance of the Congress of Berlin 27 years earlier, it provoked differing reactions. Distant German colonies such as New Guinea were given to Australia to 'manage', the remains of the Ottoman empire in the Middle East were given to France and Britain as per the wartime, and highly secretive, Sykes-Picot agreement.

In reality, the inter-war years were the last hurrah for the British and French empires as American capital and banks came to dominate the world; the failed intervention against the Russian revolution laid the foundation for the Cold War, which only finally ended in 1990.

For the labour movement and the left in general, it brought lost opportunities and divisive splits as socialist and communist parties competed for much the same political space with rather different outlooks on the longer term.

For the Labour Party in Britain the seemingly permanent contradiction of support for self-determination and independence was coupled with also accepting Britain's empire role and huge levels of military expenditure. The MacDonald-led Labour Governments of 1923–24 and 1929–31 both maintained the preparedness to use military force against colonial uprisings, whilst at the same time supporting the League of Nations and with it the right of self-determination. None of that was in the Hardie tradition, nor was it in the pre-war attitudes of Ramsay MacDonald.

In many ways, the real tradition of Hardie, including his obsessive parliamentarianism, was carried on by George Lansbury who had, despite, or perhaps because of, his opposition to the Great War, been elected to parliament in 1922 (having previously lost a self-created by-election on the issue of women's suffrage in 1912). He became Party leader after the split in the party and the 1931 election debacle. His pacifism was at odds with most Labour MPs' essentially national and often pro-military, stance. Lansbury was forced to resign in 1936 after an attack by Ernest Bevin, then General Secretary of the Transport and General Workers Union.

Bevin later went on to become the post-war Foreign Secretary in the 1945 Government. He was an architect of NATO and a supporter of nuclear weapons, who helped Indian independence and promoted the Cold War and colonial wars in Malaya and Kenya. The Labour Party, post-war, had a strong internationalist grouping of MPs who did question the behaviour of the Attlee Government. In Fenner Brockway, who described himself a disciple of Hardie, there was a sturdy champion of an end to empire.

Winning the Peace

In opposition in the 1950s, some MPs, notably Brockway and Tony Benn, exposed the crimes of the British Army in the Mau Mau wars in Kenya and together founded the Movement for Colonial Freedom, now Liberation. Their support for colonial independence was vital and a genuine expression of the whole Labour tradition dating back to Hardie in the pre-First World War Parliaments. From 1948 onwards, the other Labour tradition of virulent anti-communism dating back to the 1920s and 1930s, manifested itself both in zealous Party discipline and the expulsion of those who undertook joint actions with communists, and with support for NATO and the Cold War.

Whilst the Government of Attlee did (secretly) develop nuclear weapons in 1949, and handed the legacy on to a rather surprised Winston Churchill in 1951, there was a strong peace element in the Labour Party. The foundation of the Campaign for Nuclear Disarmament in 1957 included many very prominent Labour figures, including a future leader, Michael Foot.

The party debate in the 1950s and right through to the mid-1980s was essentially around the Cold War. Party leaders from Gaitskell onwards adopted pro-NATO and pro-nuclear positions with, for a time, Harold Wilson and later Michael Foot, being the exceptions. The new realism of the mid 1980s reasserted a pro-NATO position and thus cemented the very close relationship with the USA.

In 1982 the Argentinian occupation of the Falkland Islands (Malvinas) resulted in Prime Minister Margaret Thatcher igniting the latent imperial tendencies in Britain and despatching a Royal Navy task force to retake the islands. The emergency debate on a Saturday morning in Parliament would have resonated with Keir Hardie, as a small number of Labour MPs pleaded for a delay and negotiation and reference to the United Nations. Despite a brave stand by Tony Benn the Labour Party supported the Government, and a year later in a post-war atmosphere of xenophobia it had its worst ever election result.

The end of the Cold War in 1990 following the demolition of the Berlin Wall and break-up of the Soviet Union brought in a brief era which could have offered the possibility of widespread disarmament and transferring military resources to peaceful purposes. Whilst this was a possibility being discussed in many think tanks and social democratic circles in Europe, the US right had a very different agenda.

Jesse Helms and The Heritage Foundation were far reaching thinkers of the right and pushed the (very willing) Reagan administration into neocolonial wars in Central America. Their thinking, and close links with the arms industry later developed into the even more ominous project for a new American century led by Paul Wolfowicz and Dick Cheney which drove both the Bush administrations.

The Balkan War and Gulf War of 1991 showed that there was a thirst for western, primarily NATO-led, interventions. The first Iraq War of 1991 was a showcase for the first post-Cold War conflict as the USA asserted its very obvious military power over Iraq with long-term consequences. Fourteen years later the invasion of Afghanistan following the attack on the World Trade Centre in New York, has left behind poverty, corruption and flows of refugees. That, coupled with the invasion of Iraq, the general war on terror and the attack on Libya has produced even greater refugee flows alongside the growth of al Qaeda and ISIS, together with offshoots such as al Shabab and Boko Haram.

A global war led by the USA on supposed targets, accompanied by severe anti-terror legislation and thinly disguised Islamaphobia, have made the world a more dangerous place – and have also led to a global peace movement.

Hardie's Unfinished Business

As one of the organisers of the 2003 anti-war demonstration in London, I was acutely aware of the broad nature of the support and the global nature of the peace movement.

Just as Hardie and his endless quest for a united peace movement tried to unite the working class, mainly in Europe against the looming catastrophe of 1914, a new generation were trying to do the same on a global scale in 2003.

The great lesson from Hardie is the crying need to unite people of very different cultures and traditions in a quest for peace. Because on the other side, in a more sophisticated form, is a re-emergence of the jingoism of 1914 with the presentation of Western cultural superiority and a more integrated global economy with obsessive need for minerals and energy.

Britain spends £35 billion per year on arms and via NATO has a global reach. Also via NATO it is committed to spending two per cent of all national expenditure on 'defence'. There is thus a built-in predilection to wars of intervention, rather than peace. As we live in a world of extremes of wealth and poverty, of hunger and food waste at the same time and extraction of natural resources at an unsustainable rate, the new colonies appear.

There may be fewer actual colonies than in 1914 but the reality of the economic relationship between the USA, Europe and to some extent China with much of Africa is essentially colonial. The refugee flows from conflict and the horrors of their deaths in desperate journeys to try and survive show just how brutal the divisions are.

Hardie was a man of very little formal education, a child labourer, Trade Union organiser and Parliamentarian. Totally self-taught, he was able to visualise the need for unity across national borders in opposition to self-serving patriotism, and also to visualise the rights of then colonial subjects to their own destinies.

Had the unity of workers across the European borders, which shimmered in 1913 and 1914, succeeded in stopping the war, millions of lives would have been saved.

Perhaps the strongest message, a century on, is that a world of peace can only come by opposing militarism, but it also needs an economic system with socialist principles, not the worship of personal wealth.

'Socialism supplies the vision and a united working class satisfies the senses as a practical method of attaining its realisation.'

CHAPTER 4

Trade Unionism: Independent Labour Representation

William Knox

Trade Unionism is Trade Unionism and Socialism is Socialism. They are two different factions, and it is a hard thing to serve God and Mammon.
—Ben Pickard, president of the Miners' Federation of Great Britain

ARGUABLY KEIR HARDIE'S greatest contribution to the development of the British labour movement was the conscious coupling of the economic and political struggle of the working class. The deeply held beliefs of major industrial players, such as miners' president Ben Pickard, on the disconnect between these two spheres of action were challenged and ultimately overcome by Hardie and other socialists in the formation of the Labour Party in 1906.

Given the ingrained attachment to Liberalism of most trade union leaders in late Victorian Britain, the achievement of independent labour representation was nothing less than an outstanding and remarkable achievement. Through unstinting agitation and propaganda, in little over 20 years a much maligned and ridiculed minority had changed the mind-set of a movement.

That transformation owed much to the persistence of Hardie's belief, in spite of setback after setback, that the problems of labour could only be resolved through the creation of a mass based party supported and financed by the trade union movement. These views were the outcome of his experiences wrought in the coal mines of the west of Scotland and the day-to-day struggle of the miners there to win a living wage; indeed, they were fundamental.

Early Union Activity

Working for a living from the age of seven and with little in the way of formal education, Hardie first went to the pits at the age of ten as a trapper – a ten-hour shift opening and closing a door in order to maintain the air supply for miners at the coal face. When he was a young man he began to achieve a kind of informal status as a spokesman for his fellow miners and this drew him into conflict with the coal-owners of Lanarkshire. Their gloves-off approach to industrial relations was a first-hand lesson to Hardie, if he needed one, of the ruthlessness of the class struggle. At the age of 23 Hardie led a delegation of fellow miners at Newarthill, Lanarkshire, to protest against the two shillings a day fall in wages in 1879. While descending to the coalface the cage was ordered back to the top of the shaft and Hardie was told by the manager that 'We'll hae nae damned Hardies in this pit'.[1] He and his two brothers, David and George, were sacked and subsequently blacklisted.

The events at Newarthill were part of a wider struggle taking place in Lanarkshire over wage cuts which led to an all-out strike in 1880. This gave a tremendous boost to union organisation, which had been decimated by employer attacks in the 1860s and '70s.[2] Huge meetings were held on a weekly basis at Hamilton and Hardie was appointed corresponding secretary of the Lanarkshire Miners' Association (LMA). However, divisions soon appeared in the ranks of the miners. A rival trade union was established – the North Lanark Miners' Association – opposed to all 'strikes and blocks'.[3] It was short-lived however. There were also sectarian divisions among the miners which fatally weakened opposition to the coal-owners. Hardie as an Evangelical Christian was opposed to the Catholic faith and from time to time criticised Irish Catholic miners as easily led and spineless tools of management. The following is fairly typical of the divisive and racist language used by Hardie to describe Irish Catholic attitudes to work and trade unionism:

> Nothing angers the miner so much during a period of as to find a fellow working at stoop where the requisites are a big shovel, a strong back and a weak brain, said fellow having been busy a few weeks before in a peat bog or tattie field and who is now producing coal enough for a man and a half.[4]

Given the extent of the divisions, the LMA and the strike action were doomed to failure and after six weeks the miners were forced back to work on the employers' terms. Hardie became responsible for union debts to local traders, who had supplied the miners with food, mainly potatoes, during what was known locally as the 'tattie dispute'.

Although the strike in Lanarkshire had failed, Hardie's talent as a union organiser did not go unnoticed and later in 1880 he was dispatched to Cumnock, Ayrshire, to organise the miners there into a county union. The first serious challenge to his leadership came in August 1881 when the miners demanded a 10 per cent increase in wages; something the coal-owners flatly refused to consider. A ten-week strike ensued, which again led to victory for the owners on their terms. The experience of failure led Hardie to the realisation that unity was strength. The owners had been able to destroy small, badly organised district unions, but the larger county unions were able to weather the industrial storms. More members meant more subscriptions and greater financial stability in difficult times. It was a natural step forward to think in terms of a Scottish union in which the independence of the county unions would be recognised, but in times of crisis it would provide mutual aid and support to those in need.

In 1886 the Scottish National Miners' Federation (SNMF) was formed with Hardie as secretary and R Chisholm Robertson, of the Forth and Clyde Valley Miners' Association, as president. The Federation's policy was to raise wages by restricting output, but the implementation of this was problematic since, as Alan Campbell points out, 'there was no unanimity as to how to achieve this among the county unions'. Union support seriously declined and in just under a year membership of the SNMF fell by 10,000 to from 23,750 to just 13,000.[5]

Judging by his record, Hardie's career as a union organiser could hardly be described as successful. Outside the west of Scotland he was little known and his ideas regarding union organisation and tactics were unpopular. At the founding conference of the Miners' Federation of Great Britain (MFGB) in 1889 he stood for election to the national executive, but came nearly bottom of the list, attracting only 18 votes.[6] But Hardie was able to use his leadership of the Ayrshire miners to attend the Trades Union Congress (TUC) and begin to carve out a national reputation for himself and win an audience for his belief in independent labour representation. Given the bitter experiences in the west of Scotland of industrial disputes he had arrived at two main conclusions: firstly, that the employers were too powerful and if the issue of wages and hours were to be addressed it could only be achieved through state intervention; and, secondly, to achieve this the miners must operate outside the framework of the Liberal Party.[7] As he put it in a direct appeal to the miners in the aftermath of the 1894 miners' strike:

> All through the strike the forces of the law were used to protect blacklegs and to imprison those who even dared to look at them, or say boo to them. Honest Labour struggling for a living wage, was batoned and imprisoned whilst blacklegs were protected and glorified into the saviours of Society. The Press of the Country was against you... The Government, when appealed to, either pleaded that it could do nothing, or took the side of your opponents. The pulpit was with few exceptions hostile to you. To sum up:– on the one side were the miners, their wives and children; on the other, fighting against you, were hunger, the masters, the law, backed by policemen and soldiers, the Government, the press and the pulpit all arrayed against you. There is but one answer. Don't forget your trade union... Be a consistent member; pay your contributions regularly; loyally carry out the decisions of the union. But after you have done all this, carry your principles to their logical conclusion by acting politically as you do industrially. It is foolish to form a union to fight the coalmasters and then send one of masters or his friend to make laws for you. The class which makes the laws can do as it pleases.[8]

To act politically involved shifting the mindset of the labour movement; a huge endeavour which in essence meant taking on the highly conservative and respectable leadership of the main craft unions – coal, cotton and engineering.

Slaying The Giants

Labour leader John Burns' description of the delegates to the 1890 TUC Conference provides an indication of the uphill task ahead of Hardie:

> The 'old' delegates differed from the 'new' not only physically but also in dress. A great number of them looked like respectable

city gentlemen with very good coats, large watch-chains and high hats – and in many cases were of such splendid build and proportions that they presented an aldermanic, not to say a magisterial, form and dignity.[9]

Undaunted by these pompous and self-important labour aristocrats, Hardie in his first visit as a delegate to the TUC in 1887 aimed his attack at the very pinnacle of the craft establishment – Henry Broadhurst, who had been secretary of the parliamentary committee for 12 years and an under-secretary of state in the Liberal Government. He accused Broadhurst of having supported a Liberal by-election candidate who was a noted employer of sweated labour.[10] Although shouted down and ridiculed, Hardie's call for a new style of union leadership divorced from the boss class and the Liberal party gradually began to take root among the delegates, particularly those representatives of the unskilled workers who had played a major part in forming the more militant 'new unions' of the 1880s and '90s. But even among the craft unions, technological changes affecting the distribution of skills, the intensification of workplace discipline and the increasing involvement of the state in industrial affairs began to politicise the previously unpoliticised.[11] Such was the political progress Hardie made, that in 1893 the TUC agreed to establish a fund to assist independent labour candidates at local and national elections. However, Hardie's desire to see the elected MPs act independently in Parliament was defeated. Moreover, there was no action to establish a fund to support independent labour candidates.[12] This was a blow to Hardie, since his decision to form the Independent Labour Party (ILP) in Bradford in 1893 was made on the back of the Dockers' Strike and the successful industrial campaigns of the miners in the late 1880s and early '90s to raise wages. It was still the case that leading trade unionists pledged their support to the Liberal Party. Indeed, it was the miners and textile workers who proved to be the biggest obstacles to the growth of an independent party of the working class. There were two reasons for their opposition. Firstly, the textile workers of Lancashire and Yorkshire were Tories due simply to the fact that their employers were among the leading Liberal Party members in those parts of Britain. Voting Tory was a way of waging the class war, although admittedly in a highly unusual manner.[13] Secondly, the miners saw no need for independent representation of the working class since their geographical concentration allowed them to pretty much elect their own MPs. They saw no compelling reasons for the kind of mutual assistance advocated by Hardie and in many ways proved with the cotton spinners a major obstruction to progress.

James Mawdsley, the secretary of Cotton Spinners' Union, who stood as a Tory candidate in the 1906 General Election, got an alteration in 1895 of the TUC's standing orders to read that delegates to Congress had to be either paid officials or trade unionists working at their trade. This excluded people like Hardie and socialist agitators like Tom Mann attending as delegates. It also barred trade councils from membership – a blow at socialists who had succeeded in capturing many of them; and, lastly, the old system of voting by delegates was replaced by a 'card vote' or 'bloc vote' based on aggregate membership.[14] It is rather ironic that the conference bloc vote continually depicted in the right-wing press as a form of left-wing gerrymandering was historically the brainchild of a Tory in order to reduce socialist influence within the TUC.

The miners continued to give support to the Liberals; indeed, in the Barnsley by-election of October 1897, the ILP candidate, Pete Curran of the Gasworkers, experienced what can only be described as a political baptism by fire. At one mining village he was 'driven away by a hail of stones from the miners', who gave their votes to a mine-owner who favoured the eight-hour day.[15] Opposition was also experienced in other parts of the country. WE Harvey, leader of the Derbyshire miners, saw the ILP as a party of 'wreckers and snatchers' and refused to speak at any meeting which included Hardie.[16] In Scotland the only miners' branch affiliated to the ILP in 1905 was Lochgelly, Fife; moreover, the party's presence in Ayrshire and Lanarkshire was 'limited'. In Durham one activist said that in 1900 'the ILP was little more than a rumour amongst us'; in Northumberland too there was little ILP activity in the coalfields and it was only in 1905 that party branches began to appear.[17] There was however some room for optimism. The engineering union was coming round to the idea of independent labour representation as a consequence of their bruising defeat by the employers in the 1897 lock out. Many of the new unions formed in the late 1880s and early nineties had also taken a battering from the employers and the courts which threatened their very existence. In 1898 James Grady, president of the TUC, in his speech to Congress called for the establishment of an independent labour party and the payment of a levy of one penny a week from all trade unionists. In response to Grady's call to arms Hardie and his supporters convened a meeting at the London office of the *Labour Leader* and drafted a motion to be put to the 1899 TUC for a conference of all trade unionists, co-operatives and socialist societies to discuss 'ways and means for securing the return of an increased number of Labour members to the next Parliament'.[18] The motion was carried by 546,000 votes to 434,000 and the Labour Representation Committee (LRC) was born.

However, the inaugural meeting of the LRC at Memorial Hall, Farringdon Street, London, in February 1900, was predictably boycotted by the miners and the cotton spinners. Thomas Ashton of the latter body disdainfully predicted prior to the conference that 'not one in 10,000 trade unionists will give a moment's consideration to such a proposal' for an independent party.[19] Indeed, about half the workers affiliated to the TUC, as well as the co-operative movement, also joined the boycott. Those union delegates and others who did attend agreed to the 'idea of a distinct Labour group in the Commons with its own policies and whips'. However, the new body was an alliance between ILP and the TUC not a political party but

a federation in which the trade unions participated as organisations... it became a constituent part of the trade union movement, although with a separate existence and an independent power of decision'.[20]

Once its candidates were elected 'they would co-operate with other parties who supported labour legislation'.[21]

Agreeing in theory to support independent labour candidates at elections was one thing, but to put into effect this principle was another matter. The reality was that union members were reluctant to pay higher subscriptions for political representation. The maximum financial contribution of affiliating bodies was only 10 shillings per 1,000 members – the income that this generated in the first year of the LRC was just £210, or £4 a week. Indeed, the LRC was starved of resources and in the 1900 General Election was only able to issue four circulars at the cost of £33. Out of 15 LRC candidates only two were successful, Hardie in Merthyr Tydfil and Richard Bell at Derby, both in double-member constituencies, and elected only because of local Liberal support. Once in the Commons, Bell voted as a Liberal and in 1903 completely severed his connection with the LRC.[22]

Things were no better north of the border. Hardie had convinced co-operative societies, socialists and trade unionists there to establish the Scottish Workers Parliamentary Elections Committee (SWPEC) a month before the LRC. The SWPEC sponsored radical journalist AE Fletcher in

Calmachie, Glasgow, and although he polled 3,107 votes he did not win the seat. It also sponsored Bob Smillie, president of the Scottish Miners' Federation, in the North East Lanarkshire by-election of 1901, but he too was defeated. Moreover, the Scottish ILP had very few members. One calculation puts membership at only 1,250 in 1900.[23]

Taff Vale and Beyond

Events beyond the control of Hardie and the LRC conspired to convince the Lib/Lab leaders of the need for independent labour representation. The Taff Vale judgement of 1901–02 which put the resources of every trade union engaged in industrial action at the mercy of hostile employers rapidly improved the prospects of the LRC in a way that no amount of socialist proselytising could achieve. Affiliated membership grew from 375,000 in February 1901, to 469,000 a year later, and in 1903 to 861,000.[24] Some of the big unions such as the textile workers and the engineers were firmly on board. There was also success for LRC candidates in a series of by-elections in 1902 and 1903. This laid the basis for the MacDonald/Gladstone electoral pact in 1906 which saw 29 Labour MPs elected and the formation of the Labour Party. However, it was clear that the Labour Party was prior to 1918 little more than a trade union pressure group in parliament. It was also manifestly far from being a socialist party. As the party's historian GDH Cole stated:

> Right up to 1914 the Labour Party neither stood, nor professed to stand, for Socialism. There were... Socialists in its ranks... But [also] in its ranks were quite a number who neither were, nor called themselves Socialists; and behind these men were the trade unions.[25]

The creation of this broad alliance of middle-class intellectuals of the Fabian Society, socialist societies and the trade unions was the singular and perhaps greatest achievement of any Labour leader in Britain then or since. Hardie may, as John Burns once said to him, have been the 'leader who never won a strike, never organised a Union, governed a parish, or passed a Bill',[26] but without his vision and determination this remarkable, peaceful political revolution which would see the Labour Party take office as early as 1924 would never have come to fruition.

What then is Hardie's legacy for the modern day Labour Party, particularly at this moment in time when the leadership has been actively trying to sever the historic link with the trade unions; the strategy laid out in Ray Collins' 2014 report, *Building a One Nation Labour Party*, seems to be to build a mass participatory political party in which trade unionists voluntarily rather than automatically affiliate to Labour as individuals and not as members of affiliated organisations.[27] This would end the power of the bloc vote of unions at party conferences and greatly reduce the influence of individual trade union leaders in the area of policy. The problem of financing the party would be overcome by individual subscription. Pursuing this strategy would counter the Tories' claim of the Labour Party being the poodle of those trade unionists on the left of the political spectrum: red in this context would be dead.

Hardie never lived to witness or participate in a Labour Government and never faced the realities of power which often demand the making of choices that are inconsistent with one's values. However, he did recognise that in an imperfect world compromises had to be made and that building a coalition or alliances of progressive forces was necessary if Labour was to achieve political success. An example of this lay in rejecting in 1893 the call for the ILP to be called the Socialist Labour Party, as it was thought the word 'socialist' would have hindered the new organisation's political development.[28] For Hardie, then, Labour was a broad church (and that is in keeping with present Labour strategy), but crucial to its progress and development were the trade unions. To develop historical amnesia regarding the origins of the party; to sever links with the unions as representatives of the economic and political aspirations of the workers; to use Tory rhetoric regarding 'one nation' would have alienated Hardie. What he would have recognised was that in spite of the profound economic and social restructuring that has occurred since the 1970s in Britain, the core values of democracy, fairness and social justice which have dominated working-class political culture since the late 18th century remain potent symbols on which to establish and fashion a political constituency. Arguably, the six million votes lost by Labour since 1997 have been the result of the party's complicity in the decline of trade unionism since 1979. The use of parliamentary legislation and the law courts by the state and hostile employers have effectively ended the closed shop, the sympathetic strike, mass picketing and have rendered other aspects of the mentality of collectivism redundant. A case can be made to strengthen trade unions rather than add to the process of fragmentation and decline. Hardie, whose political awakening was the result of engagement in the day-to-day struggles of the miners for a decent wage, would have been the first to recognise this.

'...to secure the collective ownership of the means of production, distribution and exchange...'

CHAPTER 5

The ILP: Keir Hardie, Evangelist and Strategist

Barry Winter

I AM FORTUNATE to have known two ILPers who as children met Keir
Hardie. From Waltham Forest, Bert Lea recalled how Hardie had once
given him a penny to sell copies of his paper, the *Labour Leader*. Bert
continued to do this for the rest of his long life: so that penny proved
to be a good investment! From Bradford, May Allinson was among the
children performing at a special concert for Hardie at the ILP's Coming
of Age Conference in 1914. She was so inspired by his speech calling
upon his young audience to 'Live for that Better Day', that she gave a
lifetime's commitment to the ILP and to the Socialist Sunday School.

Perhaps Hardie's ability to connect with the young was born from
his own difficult and impoverished childhood. He was eight years old
when he started work to support the family. Two years later and for
the next 16 years, he was employed in coal mining, with all the dangers
this entailed. Certainly these formative experiences were etched into
his character, into his early trade union activity and into his politics,
as he progressed from being a Liberal to becoming a socialist. But his
affinity with the young was only part of the picture. Hardie displayed
a genuine affection for working people across the length and breadth
of Britain, in Europe, Japan and the Americas and also for the British
empire's subject peoples. For 25 years he spared no effort in taking his
political message to audiences, often massive, to demand social justice,
full employment, a minimum wage, an end to child poverty, a national
health service, votes for women, slum clearance, collective ownership,
opposition the Boer War and the First World War.

His record shows that first and foremost, Keir Hardie was a passionate, unstinting and unstoppable, political evangelist. His continuing engagement in the struggle to win hearts and minds for a socially

just society won him great respect from his audiences (except when he opposed war). It also made him many political enemies who viewed him as a dangerous extremist. For decades he was subjected to a stream of abuse from a hostile press, particularly after he was elected to Parliament. As soon as Hardie rose to speak in the Commons, the dark mutterings against him would begin. A future Tory Home Secretary denounced him as 'a leprous traitor'. A Welsh Liberal wrote that politicians like Hardie were 'corrupting working people' and 'lowering the tone of the citizenship of my countrymen'.

His political apprenticeship began as a miners' union official in the Ayrshire coalfield. Here he was to learn how resistant the Liberal Party could be towards selecting working-class election candidates, himself included. He also became deeply angered by the scant sympathy shown by Liberal politicians to the suffering in mining communities. As a result, he began to view the Liberals with profound distrust. This was reinforced by the Liberals' evasiveness about the call for an eight-hour working day. He concluded that it was vital to create independent political agencies for social change. The radical evangelist had also become a deeply committed political strategist.

Hardie played a leading role in establishing the short-lived Scottish Labour Party in 1888, followed by the Independent Labour Party in 1893, and eventually the Labour Representation Committee in 1900. A year before the founding of the ILP, he was elected as an independent labour MP for West Ham South. Defeated in the General Election three years later, he won the seat in Merthyr Tydfil in 1900, which he represented until his death in 1915. In addition to the *Labour Leader*, he founded and edited two other papers, *The Miner: A Journal for Underground Workers* and the *Merthyr Pioneer*, all as means of spreading the political message. He did try to set up a socialist daily paper, but that proved too difficult even for him.

The ILP

Set against this broad background, this chapter explores Keir Hardie's influence as a political strategist. In particular, the decisive roles he played in establishing both the ILP and the Labour Party. For the rest of his life, he engaged with the opportunities – and indeed the tensions – involved in sustaining the creative linkage between them. In certain respects, his experiences prefigure many of the challenges that generations of Labour lefts have faced in relation to the broader party – not least, the disappointments.

In the late 19th century the two-party system, dominated by the Conservatives and the Liberals both locally and nationally, was beginning to fracture. The gradual expansion of the franchise to working-class men was part of that process. Not all workers supported the Liberal Party (particularly in Tory textile districts of Lancashire) but 'Lib-Labism', as it was known, was widespread. It also saw a handful of working-class men entering Parliament who loyally supported the Liberals.

Initially, so did the Fabian Society. Founded in 1884, the society was dominated by a London-based, middle-class elite, which saw itself as the intellectual pioneer for a better society. The Liberal Party was its chosen political agency and it was dismissive of very idea of a party of labour. At the other end of the spectrum, revolutionary socialist parties, defining themselves as Marxist, were emerging committed to insurrectionary change. The period was also marked by increasing industrial unrest, the New Unionism, and growing international competition.

Into this flux the ILP was born. As historian Edward Thompson writes:

The ILP grew from the bottom up; its birthplaces were those shadowy parts known as the provinces... When the two-party political system began to crack, a third with a distinctly socialist character emerged... amongst the mills, brickyards and gasworks of the West Riding.[1]

This is best exemplified by the fierce industrial struggle that took place in Bradford in 1890–01 at the Manningham Mills. Facing severe wage cuts 5,000 workers, mostly women, went on strike. After five long, hard hungry months, they were defeated and driven back to work. While they had received solid support from socialists and trade unionists, they were confronted by the complete hostility of Bradford City Council. Liberal councillors as well as the Tories backed the employers. The council even called out the military to break up a public meeting. As a result, the strike leaders concluded that they needed their own independent party. First they set up the Bradford Labour Union, which soon became the Bradford Independent Labour Party.

Labour clubs began to spring up over the city and, as a result, Bradford was chosen as the birthplace of the national ILP. Presiding over the founding conference, attended by some 120 delegates, was Keir

Hardie. Among those present were members from already established branches of the ILP. Like Hardie, and in contrast to some on the left, the conference wanted the new party to be broad-based. Notably, it was the first political party to have women members on the same basis as men. It also welcomed trade unions and trades councils, campaigning organisations and labour clubs. Again in line with Hardie's thinking, the party adopted a socialist programme, including the collective ownership of production and land. However, its name was designed to reach out to wider audiences, defeating a move to identify it as an explicitly socialist party. In her biography of Hardie, Caroline Benn writes:

> The new movement was a product of many minds but it had Hardie's stamp. It was to be evangelising, with a massive national membership inclusive rather than exclusive, and only loosely organised by a National Administrative Council.[2]

She adds that it was not just a party but for many it was a 'great socialist fellowship' and that in 'setting up the ILP for others, Hardie had also fashioned it for himself'.

That did not always mean everything was always sweetness and light. Members still fell out and had fierce disagreements, Hardie included. However, the new party, derided by its critics as the Impudent Little Party, began on a creative and optimistic note.

Nor was it narrowly political. As the historian, David Howell puts it, 'The ILP was not so much a party, more a way of life.' Members also wanted to embed their vision of a better society within a very broad range of cultural, educational and social activities: to borrow Gandhi's phrase 'to be the change they wished to see.'[3]

That passionate moral fervour was very much in keeping with Hardie's outlook and helps explain his deep and abiding affection for the ILP. Despite the ups and downs, it remained closest to his heart.

The ILP's early optimism was soon to take a hard knock in the 1895 General Election. Here the wider political reality proved far more resistant to change than many of its youthful members had imagined. Not only did Hardie lose West Ham but none of the ILP's 28 candidates was successful. The leading Fabian Beatrice Webb wrote with some pleasure, 'The ILP has completed it suicide. Its policy of abstention and deliberate wrecking has proved to be futile and absurd.'[4] Another Fabian, the playwright George Bernard Shaw, thought otherwise, noting that the new party had polled 44,594 votes. Hardie's practical conclusion was the ILP 'must learn how to fight elections.'

He was not entirely sorry to lose his seat in the Commons, however, admitting that he felt 'a sense of relief... at having been released from three years' of solitary confinement.' He had certainly fought his political corner there. So much so that he was dubbed 'Member for the unemployed'. This was first used as a term of abuse, but he bore the title with pride. One thing he did hope was that if he was to be returned to Parliament, he did not want to be so politically isolated. However, he had no illusions about the limitations of the parliamentary system. As he said on another occasion: 'Parliament responds to pressure, not to arguments.' For him, that meant stirring up militant activities in the constituencies. As both a radical and a pragmatist, he sought to transform rather than overthrow the state. But that meant more than merely seeking political representation in the Commons.

The Labour Alliance

The ILP's reception during the 1895 General Election and in the Barnsley by-election brought to the fore Hardie's other goal: the need to build a broad-based alliance with the trade unions to break the Liberal Party's hold. This meant calling for a 'labour alliance' at the Trade Union Congress (TUC). On several occasions, he had tried to do so but without success. Indeed, it resulted in him being prevented from attending future TUC meetings.

The parliamentary committee of the new Scottish Trade Union Congress (STUC), chaired by his close childhood friend, fellow ILPer and miners' leader Bob Smillie, had called for trade union support for working-class parties. Hardie was allowed to participate in proceedings and at the STUC's third annual conference he gave a ten-minute speech on the need for labour representation. A motion was then passed in favour of independent parliamentary representation.

At the 1899 Trade Union Congress the resolution calling for the formation of the Labour Representation Committee was adopted. The historic motion was proposed by ILPer Tom Steels of the Doncaster Branch of the Amalgamated Society of Railway Servants (later the National Union of Railwaymen). The coal and cotton unions strongly opposed the proposal, but it was backed by many of the newer, smaller and more radical unions.

After the decision, it became widely accepted that there was something inevitable about the result, perhaps even Hardie felt this way. But this approach diminishes the scale of his – and the ILP's – persistence and achievement. Kevin Morgan writes that his

> directing role was clearly a crucial one. Without the unique combination he showed of personal charisma and close-quarters flexibility, it is difficult to see the link between the trade unions and the socialist societies being so easily established. He and the ILP were the decisive instruments in forging the common front.[5]

Over 100 trade unions attended Labour's founding conference, together with the ILP, the recently converted Fabian Society and the Social Democratic Federation (SDF). The SDF called for the 'recognition of the class war' and for the 'the socialisation of the means of production, distribution and exchange.' Not surprisingly, this was defeated.

It was Keir Hardie who moved the successful resolution defining the party's purpose as being the establishment of 'a distinctive Labour Group in Parliament.' This was as far as the trade unions were prepared to go. While it represented an *organisational* break from the Liberals, the *political* distinctiveness sought by Hardie was a long way from being achieved. Membership of the party was indirect: either through an affiliated trade union or one of the socialist societies (although the SDF did not tarry long). The ILP and the Fabians also had representation on the party's national executive but the unions had a clear majority. Likewise the block vote gave the unions the dominant voice at party conference. However, the ILP did provide the main channel for people joining the party at a local level (until Labour's constitutional reforms of 1918 when individual membership was established).

The General Election of 1906 saw some 40 LRC candidates elected, including Ramsay MacDonald (who, only 18 years later, was to become Labour's first Prime Minister) and Philip Snowden (who became the Chancellor of the Exchequer). Both were ILPers. That year, the Labour Representation Committee simplified its name to the Labour Party. Hardie was no longer alone but even the modest electoral gains raised issues about the nature of the relationship between Labour's parliamentarians and the wider party. In addition, the former Lib-Lab MPs were now officially Labour MPs but their politics remained the same. To add to his travails, Hardie was elected chairman of the parliamentary party, a role for which he was ill-suited given his general discomfort with parliamentary proceedings. MacDonald, who

Caroline Benn depicts as the outsider who wanted to be an insider,[6] was comfortable with his role as secretary of the parliamentary party, doing electoral deals with the Liberals, and generally operating in the Palace of Westminster. Hardie remained and preferred being an outsider.

In the 1906 General Election, the Liberals were returned to power after a decade in opposition, winning 400 seats. Their programme clearly sought both to respond to the emergence of the Labour Party and to retain its own working-class support. It included measures to tackle unemployment, poverty and ill health, and the introduction of old age pensions. While these were a highly diluted version of what Hardie saw as vital changes to enhance the lives of the majority, the Labour Party largely backed them. What the Liberals would not contemplate, however, was supporting workers in industrial disputes.

Labour's lacklustre performance in the Commons in these early years deeply depressed Hardie. Even the modern Labour Party's website, Our History, fully acknowledges that Labour in Parliament at this time was 'hanging from the coat-tails of the Liberals'. (Hardie himself receives only one cursory mention in this supposed 'history'.) Whenever the opportunity arose, Hardie would be either campaigning or travelling.

Hardie remained deeply critical of the Labour Party's political timidity. So much so that on one occasion he was moved to write:

> I grow weary of apologising for the state of things for which I am not responsible... There are times when I confess to feeling sore at seeing the fruits of our toil being garnered by men who never were of us, and even now would trick us out.

Still, he was not going to let go. Many ILPers shared Hardie's discontent with the Labour Party and its parliamentarians. So when in 1907 the flamboyant political maverick Victor Grayson stood in the by-election in the Colne Valley against the wishes of the Labour Party, the local ILP supported him, as did Hardie. Grayson won the seat. He soon proved to be a politically divisive figure. He tried to channel the ILP's discontent with the Labour Party into direct opposition to Hardie himself, among others. Grayson even refused to share a public platform with Hardie. This demonstrated to many ILPers that this was going too far. The tensions also led to Hardie resigning from the ILP National Administrative Council, along with MacDonald and Glasier, in 1913. They wanted to make the point that the ILP could have been more supportive of them during the dispute with Grayson. Some years later,

Grayson disappeared from the political scene but not before he had backed Britain's involvement in the First World War.

In the 1910 General Election, the Liberals were returned to office. However, this was a time of growing industrial discontent which sharpened the gulf between the Government and many working people. These disputes brought Hardie into direct conflict with the then Liberal Home Secretary, Winston Churchill. When workers at the colliery in Tonypandy went on strike for the same rates of pay as other miners in the locality (basically, the minimum wage), the Government sent in the police. Later it despatched the cavalry to patrol the streets. Hardie denounced these actions, accusing the Liberals of siding with the employers and of militarism. Churchill called him a 'disgrace'. The following year, several miners were shot by the army in two other disputes. Again, Hardie stood almost alone in Parliament in condemning these actions. His earlier hope of being less politically isolated in the Commons remained largely unfulfilled.

The First World War and Beyond

The outbreak of the First World War highlighted deep political differences within the labour and socialist movement. The trade unions and Labour Party backed Britain's involvement (although MacDonald did not) and later Labour was to enter the wartime coalition. In vain Hardie called for workers internationally to take strike action to prevent the bloodshed. The ILP was also strongly opposed the conflict and, when wartime fever was at its height, its public meetings attracted fierce public hostility. The Glasgow offices of the *Labour Leader* were set on fire.

The party was also at the forefront of contesting conscription which was introduced in 1916 – and many of its members were jailed for refusing to take up arms. But, by then Keir Hardie was dead, broken by what was happening. Never had he imagined that workers from different countries would so willingly slaughter each other at the behest of their governments.

Still despite the tensions, the links between the ILP and the Labour Party survived the war. After 1918 Labour began to attract increasing electoral support, even holding office between 1924–26. The ILP's parliamentary presence also strengthened in this period. But, this raised the question of where its MPs loyalties lay. Were they to be subject to the Labour Party's whip or free to act in accord with the ILP's more radical politics?

In 1918, under the guidance of the Fabian Society, the Labour Party also rewrote the constitution which included the Clause IV commitment to public ownership. For some, like Philip Snowden, this put into question the continuing need for a separate ILP. In the 1920s, there was a strategic attempt from the ILP to develop a constructive relationship with the Labour Party while also keeping alive the radical vision. However, widening political disagreements led to the ILP's unfortunate disaffiliation in 1932 led by Jimmy Maxton MP (with the ILP returning to the party as Independent Labour Publications in 1975).

Reconstructing Labour

At a time when the two-party system is again becoming increasingly unstable, drawing conclusions from Hardie's political experiences over a century ago poses a challenge. However, it is worth at least trying to see whether his successes and failures offer guidance to the democratic left today.

It seems to me that a progressive left still needs its evangelists and its strategists. Hardie's life shows how well he combined both roles. However, once the Labour Party was formed, his strategic vision became less clear; perhaps declining health and premature ageing, plus the sheer pressure of events, made this increasingly difficult.

That said, he opposed the temptation that many felt to break away from Labour because of its limitations. He recognised it was needed to make connections with the wider society which was so often in thrall to hostile, dominant ideologies. He also managed to avoid the lure of the parliamentary politics that has seduced so many others. Labour's electoral politics is itself always inclined to encourage short-term politics at the expense of longer-term goals. Even sustaining a coherent left-wing presence in the Labour Party has often proved difficult – and, at times, it was impermissible. Subsequent leaders of the Labour left have continued to face the difficulties of being strategists and evangelists with varying degrees of success.

But what is needed today? First, we have to restore both a clearer vision and a sense of purpose to Labour's politics and to our own. The Labour left could usefully take the initiative by encouraging the party to step back from the day-to-day pressures and deliberate on how best to reconstruct itself. There needs to be a broad and inclusive dialogue, a Big Conversation (to steal David Marquand's term), about how to respond to a society where so many feel disenchanted, disempowered and insecure. Not only do we have to re-democratise the party but we need to democratise the way Labour acts in local government and in national office. This also suggests the need for a new constitutional settlement.

So to conclude, perhaps we should sometimes remind ourselves what we are meant to be about. In this respect, Keir Hardie's political life and ethical socialism can serve as a beacon for us. And, as he was among the first to recognise, we have to inspire the next generation. That's what he was trying to do at that ILP conference in 1914 when speaking to the young people gathered there.

Here, Fenner Brockway, later to be jailed for refusing to fight, records what took place:

> Hardie was speaking. Suddenly he turned to the children and addressed them directly. I was sitting near the children and saw his face; never during all the times I had heard him speak had I seen it like this – the glow of his face was unearthly...
>
> He appealed to them to love flowers, to love animals, to love their fellows, to hate injustice and cruelty, never to be mean and treacherous to their fellows, always to be generous in service. He pictured the loveliness of the unspoiled world and the loveliness of the world as it could become. He told them how unnecessary are poverty and war and how he had tried to pass on to them a world where happiness and peace would be theirs. He and those who had worked with him had failed, but they – they, the children – could succeed.[7]

Then Hardie concluded: 'If these were my last words I would say them to you, lads and lasses. Live for that better day.'

'The "half angel, half idiot" period is over in the woman's world. She is fighting her way into every sphere of human activity.'

CHAPTER 6

Women's Suffrage: Unfailing Support

Fran Abrams

THE PHRASE, 'if Keir Hardie were alive today' has resonated through the decades within Labour Party circles. It has been a mantra both for traditionalists and for modernisers. In death, as in life, Hardie has remained a huge figure. Sylvia Pankhurst, his friend, lover and greatest fan, said that in his darkest hour he 'seemed to loom over us like some great, tragic ruin.'[1]

Hardie's name has been less closely associated with the women's movement, despite the fact that he devoted huge amounts of energy to the cause of women's suffrage. Why did he do so? What was it in his background, in his nature, that made him a champion not just of votes for women but of the rather narrow line peddled by the Women's Social and Political Union (WPSU)? For although the suffrage issue remained just one of a clutch of policies close to Hardie's heart, it was one to which he clung with particular ferocity. Indeed, it was one for which he was even prepared to compromise his socialist ideals. Throughout the years of the suffragette campaign, Hardie was one of very few key figures in the labour movement who stuck by the militants. He did so even when he was vilified by the WPSU for his connections with a party less than committed to the women's cause. There must have been more in this than pure ideological zeal. What were the personal, the psychological reasons for Hardie's attachment to this cause?

James Keir Hardie was a man who liked strong women. He was the first son of an impoverished but ambitious mother, Mary Kerr, or Keir. He never knew his father and was looked after by his grandmother while his mother worked. He enjoyed the unmitigated adoration of both women. As one biographer puts it, 'if Freud be correct that the man who is his mother's favourite conquers the world, Hardie started

87

with a stunning lead in the great Oedipal drama'.[2]

Hardie's role as an official for the Miners' Union first brought him into contact with the Pankhursts, a family who were to feature large in his political and personal existence. In 1888 he travelled to London to attend a week-long International Workers Congress, and it was there he met Emmeline and her husband Richard. The couple's radical views attracted Hardie, but there may also have been a more immediate personal bond. A year earlier the Hardies had lost a daughter, Sarah, to scarlet fever, and even more recently the Pankhursts' young son Frank had died of diphtheria. But it was politics that was to forge a lasting friendship between them, and in particular Richard's passion for women's suffrage. The Pankhursts and their associates opened Hardie's eyes to the possibility that women might not just vote, but might become as deeply involved in politics as men. Up until that time Hardie's political landscape had been almost entirely populated by men but now he met a host of political women: Annie Besant, the social reformer who championed the cause of the match girls during their famous strike, Eleanor Marx, daughter of Karl, and most important of all, Emmeline Pankhurst herself.

It was not long before Hardie was mentioning votes for women in his speeches – particularly after he was elected to Parliament as MP for West Ham in 1892. But during the 1890s the suffrage campaign was in the doldrums, and other issues cemented Hardie's relationship with the Pankhursts. He supported Emmeline during a struggle over a ban on public meetings at Boggart Hole Clough in Manchester, and was summonsed for his trouble. While he badgered ministers at Westminster over locked-out shoe workers in Leicester, the Pankhursts were on the streets there pleading the same cause. When Hardie, ousted from his West Ham seat in 1895, stood unsuccessfully at a by-election in Bradford, Emmeline rode over with her pony and trap to campaign for him. As Sylvia put it: 'Like a bit and brace, Keir Hardie and the Pankhursts seemed wrought to work in unison.'[3] Richard and Emmeline were early recruits to the Independent Labour Party, formed in Bradford under Hardie's inspiration in January 1893.

Hardie had become something of a hero in the Pankhurst household, and not just with the adults. The arrival of the *Labour Leader*, which he edited, was eagerly awaited each week, not least because Hardie wrote a column called 'Daddy Time' for its younger readers. Sylvia recalled her first sighting of the great man, sitting in the library at her parents' house, with something approaching awe:

Kneeling on the stairs to watch him, I felt that I could have rushed into his arms; indeed it was not long before the children in the houses where he stayed had climbed to his knees. He had at once the appearance of great age and vigorous youth.[4]

Differences Within the ILP

Hardie's status as an almost God-like figure in the Pankhurst household was threatened in the early days of the WPSU. In her fury at the banning of women from the new Pankhurst Memorial Hall, named in memory of her husband Richard who died in 1898, Emmeline even withdrew her regular contribution to the Keir Hardie wages fund – MPs did not receive salaries and Hardie lacked the private means on which most lived. And while Hardie remained silent on the suffrage question for several months after the foundation of the WPSU, his Labour colleagues did much to stir the women's discontent. Phillip Snowden, the Independent Labour Party's national chairman, declared that women's suffrage could only help the Conservatives. John Bruce Glasier, who had taken over from Hardie as editor of the *Labour Leader* in 1903, recorded in his diary after a meeting with Christabel and Emmeline that he had derided with scorn 'their miserable individualist sexism' and that he had told them the ILP would not lift a finger to help them. 'C paints her eyebrows grossly and looks selfish, lazy and wilful. They want to be ladies and lack the humility of real heroinism,' he added.[5] The Marxist Henry Hyndman suggested that women who wanted to vote should be exiled to a desert island.

None of this did anything to reassure the Pankhursts of Hardie's continuing friendship and support. So it must have been with some trepidation that he made his next trip to Manchester. The meeting was a tense one, but it seems Hardie handled the situation with equanimity. And where his colleagues had had little positive to say about the new organisation, he seemed unable to deny its members anything, according to Sylvia:

Votes for women? Of course! The party must be brought into line and a big campaign set on foot. A separate women's organisation? Excellent! A simple one-clause measure to give votes on the same terms as men? Certainly.[6]

Hardie even agreed to get the Independent Labour Party to publish a pamphlet by Christabel, and asked branches of the party to find out what proportion of women voters in their area would be likely to be working class – information needed to counter the argument that the WPSU aimed to enfranchise only middle-class women.

A question mark hovers over why the socialist Hardie, by now back in Parliament as MP for Merthyr, gave his unqualified support to such an organisation. The WPSU wanted votes for women on the same terms as men, and specifically *not* for all women. Even after the three great franchise reform acts of 1832, 1867 and 1884, just a third of all men had the vote in parliamentary elections.[7] The WPSU was avowedly a feminist organisation. Its demand went much further than a straightforward plea for enfranchisement; it was a demand for sexual equality. Was Hardie forward-thinking enough to attach himself to such a radical idea? On a theoretical level, he was. He argued it was valid to separate out the votes for women campaign from the struggle for full adult suffrage because it pushed the issue of gender to the fore. He also believed it was a good tactical move because it would be more easily achievable. But at heart, Hardie remained a traditionalist with his feet firmly planted in Marxist clay. If he had not had a close relationship with the Pankhursts, it is hard to believe he would have supported them in the way he did.

Socialists and Suffragettes

In the autumn of 1904 Sylvia Pankhurst left the family home in Manchester to take up a scholarship at the Royal College of Art in London. She needed a chaperone and so she would visit Hardie on a Sunday afternoon, sometimes alone and sometimes with her younger brother Harry. They would take tea at a Lyons Corner House or even have a day out in the country. Hardie, who enjoyed flirtatious relationships with a number of young women throughout his life, found Sylvia rather dour and earnest. While he would become playful, throwing stones in the air and catching them, she would look on bemused.[8] Her upbringing had been too serious, he told her. She should have had more opportunities for play. But sometimes Sylvia found Hardie strikingly unworldly. Once when she ordered coffee in a restaurant he told her he was as astonished as if she had called for a cigar – he had never tasted the drink himself. On another occasion she shocked the teetotal Hardie first by fainting in public and then by telling him he should have revived her by giving a teaspoon of brandy.

When the WPSU sent Annie Kenny to 'rouse London', Hardie was happy to help by recruiting an audience of East End women to pack the union's first big London meeting in Caxton Hall. He also helped Sylvia and Annie Kenny get tickets for a Liberal meeting at the Royal Albert Hall, in the full knowledge that they planned to stage a noisy protest. Sylvia even credited Hardie with inspiring the suffragettes to their first act of militancy. When a group of unemployed men were arrested for causing a disturbance in Manchester in summer 1905, Hardie applauded them. He told Sylvia they were 'poltroons' for agreeing to apologise to avoid imprisonment. The women noted, she said, that the government backed down soon after and implemented reforms to ease their plight: 'It was only a question now as to how militant tactics would begin.'⁹ There was support in the other direction, too. Sylvia spent many hours making big coloured posters to back the Unemployed Workmen's Bill: 'Workless and Hungry. Vote for the Bill'. During the general election of 1906, Emmeline campaigned in Merthyr, while the MP went on a grand tour around the country. Annie Kenny stayed on at Merthyr afterwards to work with women in the constituency.

Soon after the election Emmeline came to London to claim her reward for her part in his re-election – a place in Labour's list of favoured Private Members' Bills. But it was not to be. There was a stormy meeting, Hardie uncomfortable, grim-faced and silent, Emmeline voluble and angry. In fact there was little he could do – his hands had been tied by his parliamentary colleagues. Hardie promised that if he won a place in the ballot he would bring a bill for women's suffrage himself something he could not do without resigning his new position as leader of his 30-strong parliamentary party. When he failed to win a place he proposed instead to move a resolution that women should be given the vote – a procedural measure which would have no legal effect even if passed.

There was more trouble to come. Hardie had no problem with militancy at a distance, but he drew the line when it affected him personally. He was furious when Emmeline and a dozen of her suffragettes created a disturbance in the public gallery of the Commons as his suffrage resolution was debated. As she was dragged out, Sylvia saw Hardie turn angrily and stride from the chamber. But despite his fury he would not criticise the women in public. He even defended them on the grounds that the police were waiting for any excuse to throw them out.

Hardie was a traditionalist in his heart, but in his head he was a political pragmatist. In Parliament he continued to support the suffragettes, hoping for a continuation of their loyalty and backing for him personally if not for the Labour Party. When Sylvia was sent to prison he protested in Parliament that she had been convicted on the uncorroborated testimony of a single policeman. He wanted to know why Annie Kenney had been imprisoned by a magistrate who served as chief steward at the demonstration where she was arrested, and why Teresa Billington-Breig was arrested, convicted and imprisoned within a single day. Philip Snowden complained that Hardie's leadership of the party was 'a hopeless failure. Hardie never speaks to me. He seems completely absorbed with the Suffragettes.'[10]

At Labour's 1907 conference in Belfast, the suffrage question brought these tensions, and the question of Hardie's position, to a head. Much of the party wanted to keep to its belief that votes for women should mean votes for all – universal suffrage. Despite Hardie's pleadings, the conference voted for such a measure rather than supporting the WPSU's more narrowly focused aims. Fearing that the decision would force him to vote against a narrow women's bill in Parliament, Hardie used his closing speech to the conference to drop a bombshell. He threatened to resign from the party if its resolution was used to limit his support for the WPSU.

Back in Westminster the parliamentary party met to discuss the crisis and in the end a compromise was struck. A free vote would be allowed should the issue be put to a division in the Commons. But the controversy did not abate. In the *Labour Record* Fred Pethick-Lawrence wrote that the conference decision meant 'the final severance of the women's movement from the labour movement.' Within a few months all the leading figures in the WPSU had withdrawn from the Independent Labour Party. Hardie's stance had not won him friends within the WPSU, which later accused him of backsliding.

Cat and Mouse

As the suffrage struggle intensified, so did Hardie's emotional engagement with it. In September 1909, when the news came that Mary Leigh and Charlotte Marsh had been force fed in Winson Green prison, he became increasingly concerned, not least because Sylvia felt she should go to jail herself to support them. That summer he had suggested she rent a cottage in Penshurst, Kent and he visited her there as often as his schedule permitted. During one of these interludes he begged her not to go back to prison. The thought of the feeding tubes and the violence with which they were used was already making him ill – how much worse would it be if it were her? In Parliament Hardie protested that the action was 'a horrible, beastly outrage'. Some MPs laughed. Shocked by their response he wrote to the press:

> That there is a difference of opinion concerning the tactics of the militant Suffragettes goes without saying, but surely there can be no two opinions concerning the horrible brutality of these proceedings? Women, worn and weak by hunger, are seized upon, held down by brute force, gagged, a tube inserted down their throats and food poured or pumped into the stomach. Let British men think over the spectacle.[11]

Hardie received a rare plaudit from the suffragettes for his efforts over force feeding: *Votes for Women* carried a leading article by Christabel Pankhurst in which she wrote:

> Mr Keir Hardie's magnificent protest in the House of Commons against force feeding will be remembered when much that occurred in the late Parliament has been forgotten.[12]

It would, however, not be long before Hardie again upset Christabel. With the Liberal government's electoral reform bill making its way through Parliament without any promise of votes for women, Hardie made a rare departure from the WPSU line. The WPSU now wanted MPs to vote against all government bills until women had the vote, but that would mean opposing Home Rule for Ireland and several other much needed measures. Hardie refused. Christabel declared war. It was 'preposterous and insulting' that Labour should put Ireland before votes for women. She wrote in *The Suffragette*:[13]

> A women's war upon the Parliamentary Labour Party is inevitable, a war which could have been averted if the Labour Party had agreed to use their power to compel the introduction of a government measure giving votes to women.

A month later the paper launched a personal attack on Hardie, claiming he had sacrificed his principles for the sake of party unity.

In February 1913 *The Suffragette* ran a front-page cartoon bearing a picture of Hardie with a fat cigar, pushing aside a woman in his eagerness to have a friendly chat with the Prime Minister. Underneath was the comment: 'The Labour MPs have betrayed the cause of working women... They cannot be friends of the Government and friends of women too.' By now, Hardie was being heckled regularly at meetings. When the Government introduced the 1913 Cat and Mouse Act, under which suffragette prisoners who went on hunger strike would be repeatedly released and then rearrested as they recovered, Hardie protested vigorously. Just six of his Labour colleagues joined him in the 'No' lobby, while 14 of them voted for the bill. For a while, the heckling stopped.

In February 1914 a short notice appeared in *The Suffragette*, under the heading 'One Policy, One Programme, One Command'. It noted that Sylvia's East London Federation of Suffragettes was 'a distinct organisation independent of the WPSU' and added that this was merely a restatement of a situation which had existed for some time: 'Viz, that Miss Sylvia Pankhurst prefers to work on her own account and independently.' Sylvia had been thrown out of the WPSU. Hardie had just questioned the Home Secretary about hunger strikers, of whom she was one. Not long afterwards, he asked about the rearrest of Emmeline in Glasgow. As the war between Christabel and the Labour Party continued, Hardie's support was unabated. At the ILP conference that year, a party rally had to be stopped while a crowbar was fetched to separate a suffragette from the seat to which she had chained herself. When Ramsay MacDonald got up, bags of flour were thrown and the fire alarm went off. Hardie, who was in the chair, remarked mildly that he could better endure such behaviour from women than from men.

In June 1914, Sylvia, in a state of collapse after repeated hunger strikes, was carried to the House of Commons. Hardie was there to meet her, and while she lay prostrate under Cromwell's statue he went to find Asquith and persuaded him to agree to a meeting with a group of her supporters. Again, Hardie began raising questions relating to Sylvia's concerns in Parliament. Just a few days after her trip to Parliament he rose to defend one of her East End friends, Melvina Walker, who had proclaimed apropos of the suffragettes' arson campaign, that if there had been mansions to burn in the East End 'they would have been hot long ago.'

During that summer Sylvia and her friend Norah Smyth arranged to meet Hardie at Penshurst in Kent – scene of much happier times she had spent with Hardie five years earlier. As a result of this meeting, Hardie agreed to press his party colleagues to include a call for both manhood and womanhood suffrage in their next election manifesto. But other events were about to intervene. The prospect of war was looming, and the harrowing thought of it threatened to bring Hardie down completely. And if the treatment meted out to him by the suffragettes seemed cruel, it would be as nothing to what he would now have to endure from his own colleagues.

And then the War

In August 1914 Emmeline was recuperating from hunger strike in St Malo in France. The war was not unexpected but it threw into stark relief the position in which the suffrage movement then found itself. Over the past two years the atmosphere surrounding the struggle had become so tense, so extreme, that there was no way forward but death for large numbers of women. The war provided an escape route; a means of bowing out gracefully. The government had become as entrenched as had the women – neither side would be seen to give in. If the government granted the vote, it would appear to have bowed to terror tactics. If the women called an end to their activities, their struggle would appear to have been in vain. War changed everything.

Emmeline wasted no time in winding up the movement and urging her supporters to turn their energies to war work. As her friend Ethel Smyth put it, 'Mrs Pankhurst declared that it was now not a question of Votes for Women, but of having any country left to vote in.'[14]

Sylvia and her East End movement continued to demand the immediate enfranchisement of women and she supported the International Women's Peace Congress in 1915.

When Hardie died on 26 September 1915 the ILP paid for his funeral, at which the cortege was a quarter of a mile long. Although Sylvia sent a wreath in suffragette colours there were few other tributes from the women of the WPSU for whom he had toiled so long and tirelessly. It fell to Isabella Ford, a leading constitutional suffragist, to pay tribute to the work Hardie had done to promote women's suffrage:

His extraordinary sympathy with the women's movement, his complete understanding of what it stands for were what first made me understand the finest side of his character. In the days when Labour men neglected and slighted the women's cause or ridiculed it, Hardie never once failed us, never once faltered in his work for us. We women can never forget what we owe him.[15]

By modern standards, Keir Hardie was not a liberated man. His old-fashioned romanticism and his admiration for his Victorian mother left him ill-equipped for the more radical sexual politics espoused by some of his contemporaries. But he was in many ways a man ahead of his time. His devotion to the cause of women's suffrage is just one example of that, along with his opposition to the empire and his internationalism. He was also a man who, once attached to a belief, clung to it with a tenacity that had sometimes had to be seen to be believed. For that, if for nothing else, the members of the suffragette movement had much to be grateful for.

This essay is based on a chapter in: Abrams, F, *Freedom's Cause: Lives of the Suffragettes*, Profile Books, London, 2003.

'The most we can hope to do is to make the coming of Socialism possible in the full assurance that it will shape itself aright when it does come.'

CHAPTER 7

Home Rule: Socialist, Not Nationalist

Dave Watson

THE PHRASE 'HOME RULE' has been used to describe many different approaches to constitutional change. It has been claimed by nationalists seeking independence, advocates for Devo-Max and latterly Ed Miliband promising further devolution through a Home Rule Bill. The name of Keir Hardie is often used, and misused, in support of these policy positions. In this chapter I will look at Hardie and Home Rule in the context of the current constitutional debate.

This is a challenging task because, as Bob Holman puts it in his concise biography,

> in some ways, he is still an enigma. He wrote no autobiography, penned just a handful of pages in a diary, kept hardly any of the thousands of letters he must have received. On the other hand, he wrote numerous articles in papers and newspapers.[1]

I have always thought of Hardie as an agitator rather than a political theorist, as he said himself:

> I am an agitator. My work has consisted of trying to stir up a divine discontent with wrong.

Despite this, it is clear that Keir Hardie did indeed support Home Rule. One of the most popular images of Hardie is from his election poster for the Mid Lanark by-election of 1888 that includes Home Rule as the first demand. Hardie wrote in 1889:

> I believe the people of Scotland desire a Parliament of their own

and it will be for them to send to the House of Commons a body of men pledged to obtain it.

Discovering Hardie's Home Rule

Even before devolution, Scotland maintained separate institutions following the Treaty of Union in 1707 – in particular (Article 19) a separate legal system. This helped maintain a national identity and arguably a different approach to politics and government. Nineteenth century Scotland was not the centralised state it would become before devolution. The town councils were powerful bodies and Scottish local supervisory boards administered welfare, leading, as Gordon Brown states:

> The Scottish public would see the boards and the local councils, rather than the distant Whitehall and Westminster, as responsible for the routine government of Scotland.[2]

While it can be overstated, as it often is today, there was a Scottish radical tradition derived from the Presbyterian Church and the Scottish education system that reinforced the democratic principle and an element of localism. However, it could be argued that the Kirk was more theocratic than democratic and the school system meritocratic rather than egalitarian.

In the 1880s it was the Irish question that drove the Home Rule debate. While Hardie did have support from the Scottish Home Rule Association, it had little influence in Mid Lanark. Hardie was more concerned to show his support for Home Rule in Ireland given the large numbers of Irish residents in the constituency. The Irish National League provided important support to his campaign through the registration of Irish voters.

There is a conventional, if contested, view that Irish Home Rule held back the development of Labour politics during a period when sectarianism was never far from the surface. William Kenefick[3] reminds us that many Lowland middle-class Scots were resentful that the Irish had made the issue of Irish Home Rule a factor in Scottish politics. For many in Protestant West of Scotland, with its strong links to Ulster, 'Home Rule' meant 'Rome Rule'. Sectarianism wasn't of course a one-way street. Knox states that Catholic Irish miners in Lanarkshire considered 'Protestantism... more obnoxious than low wages.'[4] This would have been a real challenge for Hardie because sectarianism affected the coalfields more than any other industry.

Keir Hardie's position on Irish Home Rule must have been less than obvious to some after the formation of the Scottish Labour Party in 1888. Emrys Hughes in his biography of Hardie[5] tells the story of a meeting in the Camlachie constituency of Glasgow that had a large Irish population. Local 'roughs' invaded the meeting because, 'people did not know Keir Hardie's attitude towards Irish Home Rule.' Cunninghame-Graham, chairing the meeting, had to brandish a fake pistol to maintain order. However, they were both carried out of the hall with acclaim after Hardie spoke strongly in favour of Home Rule for Ireland.

Kenefick also points to the links between land reform and Home Rule in the 1880s. This linked back to an older, radical anti-landlord tradition that went back to the days of Chartism:

> Thoughts of socialism may rarely have troubled the average working man in Scotland, but support for land reform and home rule was popular and widespread, and through the agitations of the labour movement nationalist and internationalist sentiments developed hand in hand.[6]

Land reformers seeking broader support extended the aims of the Highland 'land war' movement to the Lowlands and in 1884 the Scottish Land Restoration League was founded. It was backed by Hardie and affiliated to the Scottish Labour Party in 1888. The more explicitly socialist Scottish Land and Labour League also affiliated in 1888. These movements popularised the idea of Home Rule and had political success. The Crofters' Party secured the election of five MPs in the 1884 election and this encouraged those who argued in favour of supporting independent candidates against official Liberalism.

Scottish Demands

Gladstone was committed to treating all nations in the same way and promised that a Scottish Home Rule Bill would follow his Irish Home Rule Bill. Gladstone's Home Rule programme was certainly not independence, as the supremacy of the Imperial Parliament would be maintained. This led to the creation of the Scottish Home Rule Association in 1886 and the conversion of Scottish Liberals to Home Rule in 1888. It also led to a split within the Liberals, with the Whigs who opposed Home Rule joining the Conservatives. Hardie welcomed this split as he assumed this would result in a more progressive Liberal Party.

Hardie was also no bystander in the Home Rule movement. He was among the vice-presidents of the Scottish Home Rule Association and Ramsey MacDonald was the Secretary of the London branch. The first Scottish Home Rule motion was introduced in the House of Commons in 1889 followed regularly by motions and first readings of bills up to the First World War. The 1913 Bill went as far as a second reading.

It might be argued that the formation of the STUC as a separate organisation to the TUC reflected a degree of nationalism within organised labour of which Hardie was rooted. However, others[7] point to the parochialism of trade unions during this period with strong district and regional structures. Centralisation only gained significant ground with new unionism in the run up to the First World War. The STUC's formation, as their evidence to the Kilbrandon Commission put it, 'reflected the uneasiness in Scottish trade union circles about the 'remoteness' of London.' However, the decision of the TUC to debar Trades Councils from participation in Congress decisions was probably more important, given the greater role they played in the Scottish trade union movement.

The STUC unanimously adopted the principle of Home Rule at the 1914 Congress, although the motion required no action. It is also clear from speeches by trade union leaders of the time that Home Rule was very different from separatism. They saw the need for a body to focus on local issues while still joining with the British and Irish congresses to promote, as Robert Smillie put it, 'the improvement of the condition of workers of the country as a whole.'[8]

This is also the period of Hardie's conversion from Liberalism to socialism, driven by the Lanarkshire miners strike and the failure of the Liberal Party to support the eight-hour clause in the 1887 Mines Bill. The founding programme of the Scottish Labour Party in May 1888 included Home Rule for each separate nationality in the British empire with an Imperial Parliament for imperial affairs. This commitment to Home Rule was seen as part of the early Labour leader's radical and Liberal heritage.

As Hardie's efforts focused on the formation of a British Independent

Labour Party (ILP), the greater engagement of trade unions put Home Rule lower on the agenda. The 1901 programme of the Scottish Workers Representation Committee (including the ILP) had no specific mention of Home Rule for Scotland. Keating and Bleiman[9] conclude that Home Rule remained part of the policy of Labour in Scotland up to 1914, but it was limited to an expression of general support. The priorities were the more important social needs of the working class and the greater integration of the labour movement on a British basis.

Hardie's own publication[10] *From Serfdom to Socialism* appeared in 1907. In it he sets out his basic principles of socialism with chapters on municipal socialism, the state, Christianity, workers and women. However, Home Rule does not feature. In fairness, the work focuses on principles rather than organisation. However, that also reflects Hardie's political approach as he says in the booklet:

> To dogmatise about the form which the Socialist state shall take is to play the fool. That is a matter with which we have nothing whatever to do. It belongs to the future, and is a matter which posterity alone can decide. The most we can hope to do is to make the coming of Socialism possible in the full assurance that it will shape itself aright when it does come.

The Home Rule campaign was reinvigorated in the period 1914–22, before a UK political strategy asserted itself in the Labour movement, leading to a permanent split with nationalism. As Richard Finlay puts it:

> Although Scottish home rule commanded a wide range of support, much of it was nominal and for those keen protagonists of the policy, the key issue was how to translate this into political action.[11]

This led to the eventual creation of the SNP. However, these events happened after Hardie's death in 1915 and so he played no role in them.

Home Rule does not appear to be a significant part of Hardie's ideology as a politician. In July 1892 Hardie had been elected as the MP for West Ham in London, although he did not entirely ignore Home Rule even in that election. He agreed with Gladstone's Newcastle Programme of 1891 and particularly stressed the Home Rule elements, although Caroline Benn points out that he later called the document a 'miscellaneous compendium of odds and ends.'[12] He also lost the support of many Irish voters because he said his support for Home Rule had been with a 'bad conscience', although that was apparently because of a proposal to set up a House of Lords there. Two local priests said he made Ireland the 'tail of a socialist programme'. Hardie could certainly see the dangers of nationalism to the working class. Both when he was in Dublin and Belfast pleading the cause of solidarity during the transport workers strike, and later during the Ulster Protestant rebellion against Home Rule. He viewed these developments as the political right protecting landed interests against the growing strength of working people.

Internationalism

Hardie certainly supported colonial emancipation. He led the British delegation at the 1904 Congress of the International at which the Indians sent a delegate for the first time. He rattled the Raj during his 1907 visit to India when he said, 'The sooner the people of India controlled their own affairs the better'. He kept the pressure up when he returned to the UK with a pamphlet called *India: Impressions and Suggestions*. However, there is no suggestion in any of these campaigns that he regarded Scotland or Wales for that matter as colonies. Caroline Benn in her conclusion puts it this way:

> How the common wealth was administered, and by what forms of democratic accountability control was exercised, were details he was often content to leave to others, though he always favoured strong local oversight and parliaments for Scotland, Wales and Ireland.[13]

Kenneth Morgan in his biography[14] of Hardie argues that while there are gaps in his version of socialism, his focus was sociological not economic and 'never hedged around by rigid dogma'. While Morgan has little to say about Hardie and Home Rule, he does point to his pamphlet, 'The Common Good' (1910) in which Hardie wrote enthusiastically about municipal reform and the ownership of transport, utilities and municipal trading. Although he envisaged that these would lead to public ownership at the national level as well. It can therefore be argued that Hardie was not a natural centraliser and explicitly opposed it – the local tradition remained important to him.

Bob Holman interprets Hardie's call for Home Rule as a call for independence. During the 2014 independence referendum, Holman argued in *The Herald*[15] that Hardie's Home Rule was the same as independence. He based this claim on Hardie's call for more working-class MPS and railing against elitism of Westminster. He also said that Hardie would have welcomed gender balance, something he campaigned strongly on. Indeed he probably would have, but that is largely due to the Scottish Labour Party's 50:50 policy, not the Parliament. Of course Hardie would have attacked privatisation and inequality, but these are political decisions not a consequence of constitutional reform.

To claim that Hardie was a nationalist is a challenging conclusion to draw from the historical evidence. His life and work had an obvious UK and broader international solidarity context. My first job as a full time union official was in South Wales. I well remember attending a meeting in Merthyr Tydfil Town Hall where there was a wonderful bust of Hardie inspirational to a young idealistic union official. More recently, Newham council in London has published an excellent booklet commemorating Hardie's time as the MP for West Ham. It is hard to imagine a Scottish nationalist politician standing for an English or Welsh constituency.

I would argue that the evidence above shows that Home Rule for Hardie was a reflection of the Liberal tradition he was part of. It certainly survived his conversion to socialism and remained part of the programme of the wider Labour movement during this period – albeit with a much lower priority. The Liberal leadership of this period was, as Tom Devine argues,[16] unenthusiastic about Home Rule and their proposals imply something closer to limited administrative reform than real self-government. The Liberal tradition, even the most radical elements, was closer to what we now call devolution, rather than independence.

The Scottish Home Rule Association was not campaigning for independence. Its Vice-Chair John Romans said, 'No Scotsman whose opinion is worth repeating, entertains for a moment, an approximation to repeal the union.'[17] This is because Home Rule was viewed as part of a distinct Scottish national identity within the wider union. Even the 1913 Government of Scotland Bill, the most advanced of the Home Rule bills, fell somewhat short of what we would call Devo-Max or Full Fiscal Autonomy today.

The Labour movement and Hardie simply had bigger priorities in this period. Challenging capital, trade union immunities and improving social conditions were the key issues. They sought common ground with workers across the UK and political reform at Westminster, rather than an independent Scotland. This culminated in the STUC and the Labour Party abandoning support for Home Rule by 1932.

Contemporary Resonance

We should always be wary about attaching views on current issues to historical figures or judging them by modern standards. For example, I recall being surprised when I visited the National History Museum in Bucharest, to discover that Vlad the Impaler was a Romanian national hero. This didn't quite fit with my images, influenced by Bran Stoker's Dracula, of the historical figure. Vlad Tepes, as he was properly known, may have engaged in violent acts, but he was a man of his times.

Hardie's thoughts on Home Rule were outlined more than 120 years ago in a very different political environment. Something nationalists and others would do well to remember. They often write[18] that Keir Hardie would be 'spinning in his grave' at the actions of the Labour Party today. If they knew anything about Hardie they would know that he won't be spinning in his grave for anything – because he was cremated!

In this year's General Election we again saw Joan McAlpine MSP use her Daily Record column[19] to argue that, 'Keir Hardie would back the SNP if he were alive today'. She is certainly correct that he wouldn't have supported drinking at football matches but, on the other hand, he would have approved of Jim Murphy's personal abstinence from alcohol – something very rare these days in a political leader, the honourable exception being the Keir Hardie Society's first Hon President, Tony Benn.

While Hardie would not support austerity, he would also be arguing for the redistribution of wealth. When Nicola Sturgeon was asked at her General Election manifesto launch to name a redistributive policy enacted by the SNP in Holyrood, she was unable to cite a single example. We have had plenty of middle-class welfarism, but relatively few effective measures to reduce inequality or poverty.

Other aspects of Keir Hardie's early manifesto are also absent from the current SNP policy programme. Hardie's no landlordism and fair rents campaign doesn't quite match with SNP MSPs' voting against rent controls. The same could be said on workers' rights and, of course, the SNP's centralising tendencies would have been unlikely to find much support from Hardie either.

In essence, the SNP is a successful broad coalition from left to right with a common goal of independence. It pursues a broadly social democratic political line – left of centre on social policy, if not always on economic policy. Keir Hardie was a socialist and the SNP emphatically isn't a socialist party. In fairness it doesn't claim to be one.

That is not to say that Keir Hardie would agree with all aspects of current Labour Party policy. He probably could sign up to the aims and values in the rule book in 2015, although he would almost certainly have been more comfortable with the pre-Blair version. The founding programme of Keir Hardie's Labour Party included the nationalisation of the railways and other means of transit (waterways and tramways), the banks, the land, all mineral rights and the abolition of the House of Lords and all hereditary offices. I fear he would also have been unimpressed by the professionalisation of MPs, a view shared with much of the electorate!

Also, he would not have been much enthused by the insertion of 'patriotic interest' into the Scottish Labour rulebook. He wrote about the abuse of patriotism during the First World War, saying:

> I conclude by calling the attention of organised Labour to the facts that Imperialism, Militarism and Patriotism have added during the past fifty years nearly £200,000,000 a year to the financial class from investments abroad... But the war will end... and the Imperialist monied property owning, ruling class who today are so proud of the patriotism of the working man, will still be supreme... Their incomes from Colonial and Foreign investments will not be touched. And everyone of those 'patriots' will once more combine their strength to keep the working man in the lowly station to which it has pleased God to call him.

His vision was 'From Serfdom to Socialism', not the SNP's manifesto slogan: 'Stronger for Scotland'.

Drawing a Lesson

While we should not apply 21st century values to a 19th century politician, there are some things we can be fairly clear about. Keir Hardie was a socialist, not a nationalist. His, and the early Labour Party's support for Home Rule was part of the Liberal tradition that was closer to what we would recognise as devolution today. Its importance declined as Hardie and the early pioneers of the labour movement focused on other priorities.

The relevance of the work of Keir Hardie is that he took the message of socialism to hundreds of thousands of ordinary people across the UK. He changed the way a generation thought about what was possible; an alternative vision of what today we would call social justice.

If there is a lesson for the Scottish Labour Party today, it is not about Home Rule, or even greater devolution, important though I believe that is, it is the importance of communicating a radical vision of what is possible. It is also not the fantasy politics of those who claim to want social justice but spend all their time attacking Labour. But neither is it the managerialism that sometimes dominates party policy. The fairer Scotland envisaged in Hardie's work is possible and Scottish Labour should be its champion.

'My first concern is the moral and material well-being of the working classes.'

CHAPTER 8

West Ham: 'A Splotch of Red'

John Callow

KEIR HARDIE ARRIVED at Parliament with a flourish. Even at the time, memories blurred and accounts conflicted.

Had he processed from West Ham to Westminster accompanied by a single trumpeter, or by massed brass bands, marching alongside his ragged constituents?

Had the strains of the *Marseillaise* or *The Red Flag* shaken the window frames and door-jambs of the Commons?

Was his wagon barred by the constables at the gate, occasioning scuffles, or did it swing across the courtyard of the Palace of Westminster in a majestic arc, before setting down its occupant on the steps?[1]

In this manner, the symbolism of the event, and its attendant mythology, seemed to have eclipsed the wider significance of the election of James Keir Hardie as the first Independent Labour Member of Parliament, and his role thereafter as a practical constituency MP who – as a lone socialist voice and representative of the poor, the excluded and disenfranchised – consistently and self-consciously articulated original, dissonant and extremely disturbing arguments at the heart of an imperial government that spanned no less than a third of the globe. It was no wonder that he struck establishment commentators as an exotic, unfathomable and extremist figure, who could be mercilessly lampooned in the press as 'queer Hardie' on account of his dress, apparent Bohemianism and counter-cultural ideas.

Yet, at the same time, his rise to prominence as the trail-blazer, moral compass and avowed leader of the British labour movement was far from assured and at times, even in the eyes of some of his own supporters, not a little incongruous.

A Lonely Voice

Beatrice Webb, for one, rejoiced in his defeat at the polls in 1895, writing him off as an insubstantial figure whose time, and notoriety, had passed. In so doing, she did much to set the tone for later writers and political historians who tended to view Hardie's parliamentary record, as MP for West Ham South, as something of an anti-climax. Political opportunities had been squandered, the pursuit of controversy had taken the place of solid achievement on behalf of the working class; his attendance and voting records were poor, and he frequently seemed out of his depth over matters of procedure and the marshalling of debate. The fiery agitator seemed to have made but a poor parliamentarian. Hardie, himself, seemed to concur in this view, lamenting that his work at Westminster had cut him off from 'communion' with his 'fellows'. London, he thought, was

> a place which I remember with a haunting horror, as if I had been confined there once in some long-ago stage of a former existence. The weary feet on the pavement, the raucous song, the jingle of the cab-horse bells and – the babble of St Stephen's [the House of Commons] jarred in his ears and unsettled his nerves.[2]

Parliament does not seem to have been his natural arena, while his engagement with his West Ham constituency appears to have been patchy and to have originated through good-fortune and an element of expediency, rather than as the product of deep, long-term commitment. He had never visited the borough until invited to stand as its parliamentary candidate in 1890; in modern parlance, it might be argued that he had been 'parachuted' into the constituency by ad-hoc local groupings of socialists, land leaguers and radical Liberals.

As with most received wisdoms, there is an element of truth in this view of Hardie's effectiveness as a parliamentarian. Yet, a closer investigation suggests something subtly different: namely, that Hardie's failure to acknowledge parliamentary conventions and to accept a dominant political culture permitted him to strengthen his position as the leading exponent of socialism in Britain, and to raise matters for Commons scrutiny – not least the scourge of unemployment – that otherwise would have gone almost completely unnoticed and unremarked, by the elites at Westminster. Hardie had, after all, intruded upon a Parliament which was not the preserve of full-time politicians, but rather of gentlemen pursuing a system of ambition, or, more occasionally a vocation, for part of the year. In an age when MPs were unpaid and expected to enjoy the benefit of private incomes, Hardie's frequent absences from Parliament owed far more to the constraints of having to earn a living outside of the House, than to a sense of antipathy or dilettantism.

Radical West Ham

West Ham appears as a particularly good fit for a trade unionist and socialist propagandist who sought to unite the industrial and political wings of the labour movement: it was a shock-centre of late Victorian capitalism, with a rich and diverse political culture, 'a little isolated republic outside the vast area of the metropolis' where the factory and dockyard owners swept their 'human rubbish'; the flexible labour of those marginalised women and men who powered and serviced the capital, concentrated in overwhelming numbers. The population had expanded rapidly as the result of new industries and the docks which drew people into the new borough where plentiful land was available to build upon, at cheap rates, and where the laws regarding the regulation of 'offensive trades' were far less severely enforced.[3] As a consequence, pollution rapidly became a fact of everyday life with the 'atmosphere... blackened with smoke and poisoned with the noxious fumes of chemicals, and the stench of bone manure and soapworks', with housing often resembling shanty towns, quickly, cheaply and poorly thrown together in order to maximise the landlords' profits.[4] Work was often casual and erratic.

In laying the foundations for Hardie's candidature, Cunninghame Graham characterised West Ham as being

> that extremist product of modern civilisation... a very microcosm of the 19th century world, street upon street of half-cooked brick abominations, falsely called houses; here and there a 'Little Bethel' chapel... Row upon row of open stalls at night, where the stale vegetable is sold under the flare of naphtha lights. Public houses not a few. An air of desolation over the whole place... On one side lines of endless docks and endless misery.[5]

The absence of a well-defined, or numerous middle-class presence in the borough may well have reinforced this sense of deprivation and immiseration; but it also left less room for patronage, deference and interference in local affairs. Thus, while both Roman Catholicism and Protestant nonconformity maintained a significant presence in the borough, they could not claim to be the dominant feature in its life. Furthermore, there was also an unusually large minority who seem to have belonged to no fixed religious denomination, or considered themselves as atheists.[6] The gaps created permitted a freedom of thought to flourish that, initially, manifested itself through a succession of radical clubs and by the late 1880s, it facilitated the spread of socialist ideas.[7]

Annie Besant, Edward Aveling and Eleanor Marx had all drawn crowds when they lectured in the area and had, after 1889, attempted to organise new trade unions among the dockers and gasworkers. Street corner meetings, agitation and paper sales were carried out across the borough by effective and extremely active teams of Social Democratic Federation (SDF) propagandists, who organised within working-class communities. Whole branches of the Gasworkers' Union were enrolled in the SDF, accepting an explicitly Marxist programme, and committing themselves to developing and promoting education for the working class. From the outset they had sought independent political representation and contested local government elections. By 1891 Will Thorne – the union's General Secretary and leading light – and six allies were elected to the council on a recognisably 'labour' ticket.[8] It made sense that where a labour group existed, a party might follow. Thorne was able to deliver industrial muscle, numbers on the ground, and considerable political acumen to the campaign, that would prove invaluable in galvanising the core working-class vote in West Ham.[9] It was a selfless act by a serious politician but it was also one that would pay immense dividends for both of the men concerned.

If the SDF had laid the foundations, and created the climate, in which a Socialist candidate could be elected; then it was the split within the local Liberal party, coupled with a personal tragedy, which established Keir Hardie as a realistic parliamentary candidate in West Ham South. The more radical Liberal faction had been unwilling to accept the imposition of a middle class candidate upon their constituency and, after the losing the seat to the Conservatives, had embarked upon the patient, painstaking and largely unremarked business of canvassing and voter registration. However, the shock suicide of their preferred candidate, James Hume Webster just six months before the election of 1892, left the Liberals without a credible candidate of their own.[10] Hardie was, thus, unexpectedly given a clear field in which to run against the incumbent, Conservative MP, Major George Banes. With hindsight, it is easy to see that Hardie presented a near perfect skill set that appealed right across the disparate radical interest groups based within the constituency. Though an outsider he was well-known to local trade unionists for his work among the Ayrshire miners and the Liberals would have recalled him running as their candidate at Mid-Lanark in 1888. Hardie's background as a charismatic lay preacher and as a champion of both temperance reform and religious dissent, recommended him to the nonconformist churches in the borough. At the same time, his Catholic Irish support recognised his longstanding, support for Home Rule in Ireland. The new socialist societies, similarly, knew and understood Hardie. He had sprung from the working class and despite his relative youth – he was in his mid-30s at the time of his arrival in West Ham – he had already established a formidable reputation for himself as a trade union leader, industrial militant, and as a powerful socialist orator and journalist.

Uncompromising Candidate

If his election address fought shy of explicitly naming a socialist credo, then the essence of socialism and Hardie's political will and objects were the hallmarks burned deeply into his manifesto for West Ham. 'I have no sympathy, whatever', he told his constituents, 'with a system which robs the nation of its wealth, acts as a drag on industry, and cheats labour of its own. I would cordially support all forms of legislation which would rid honest industry of the useless idler, whether personified in the absentee landlord, the sweating shareholder, or the gambling and swindling stockbroker. My first concern', he continued, 'is the moral and material well-being of the working classes.'[11] He advocated public ownership of the railways, the mines, the banks and the dockyards; the introduction of the old age pension; the public provision of houses for working people at low – and controlled – rents; the disestablishment of the Church of England; the taxation of land values; and reasonable limits to be set upon the working day. Hardie was speaking uncompromisingly of class politics, the redistribution of wealth, and of the eventual achievement of socialism in Britain.

Hardie's introduction to the seat had been effected by Dr John Moir, a fellow Scot and the Vice President of the Scottish Labour Party, who was working as a general practitioner in Canning. He knew the area and acted as a bridge between the Liberal and socialist groups in local government.[12] Just as importantly, he knew and respected Hardie and championed his adoption as the parliamentary candidate for the constituency. A committee representing an extremely heterogeneous alliance between the more radical Liberals, the socialists and the local branch of the Land Restoration League, sought 'their own' candidate,

> a bona fide representative of working-class interests, who in addition to being a Home Rule Liberal, will also strive to secure for labour a better share of the comforts and enjoyments of life.[13]

On the 17 April an open air meeting packed with members of the gas and dock workers unions saw his formal adoption as 'the Labour, Radical and Home Rule' candidate with the show of some 250 hands.[14]

Yet, it would be a mistake to believe that Hardie was prepared to be all things to all men. He tersely rejected help from the national office of the Liberal Party, refused to work with those local activists who had been strong partisans of the late Hume Webster, and spurned recognition as the official Liberal candidate. 'The Liberal Party', he thought,

> is endeavouring to live and flourish on what were the big issues of 25 years ago. Liberalism, even in its most advanced form, is a quarter of a century in the rear of the requirements of the times.

The political language of Liberalism no longer resonated at the popular level and Hardie understood, better than most, that a new vocabulary and a new political formation were required in order to address the needs of working men and women. His thoughts were already set upon the creation of an independent Labour Party and he viewed himself, at this stage, as simply one of a raft of 'Labour' candidates standing in the 1892 election. These included among their ranks John Burns (who was considered as their natural leader); Cunninghame Graham, Hardie's aristocratic friend and political mentor; Ben Tillett of the Dock Workers' Union; Havelock Wilson, of the Sailors' and Firemen's Union; and the redoubtable Joseph Arch, Primitive Methodist preacher, veteran radical and the inspiration behind the Agricultural Workers' Union.

In many ways, the campaign was a strange one: with Hardie's frenetic round of factory gate meetings, leafleting, and speaking engagements contrasted with a complete absence of activity, or public pronouncement, on the part of his Conservative opponent. It is not an unfair caricature to suggest that Major Banes believed himself possessed of a natural right to govern, and that the votes of propertied men would inevitably secure him a second victory in what was considered to be a safe seat for the Tories. However, the local newspaper considered that Hardie

> had got hold of the working men as no ordinary Liberal would have gripped them... he is a man of ability, sincerity, and considerable force of character. His constituents believe in him thoroughly.[15]

The result at the polls, on 4 July 1892, seemed to fully confirm this verdict with Keir Hardie taking the seat with 5,268 votes, to Major Banes' 4,036, and marking a seismic shift in British politics.[16] That night, Hardie addressed crowds of his supporters from the balcony of Stratford Town Hall and looked out over a sea of jubilant faces, union banners and red flags. The Gasworkers' band struck-up a medley of radical and French revolutionary songs and the local SDF branches celebrated until the dawn. Later, the correspondent of the *Workman's Times* recorded the effect of the tremor sent out that night from West Ham to Whitehall:

> For the first time the governors of the people, who have governed so long for their own profit, are come face to face with one of the people whom they have governed.

He thought that Keir Hardie was:

> A man who can stand and look at them from clear, honest eyes, who is not there to ape their dress and manners and affect to be ashamed of his own class, but who is there as the first of a new legislature, to whom they are slowly, perhaps, but surely to give place. A man who is there as the advance guard of an army who will render clear the meaning of the phrase that Government shall be 'of the people, by the people, for the people.'[17]

Isolation in Parliament

However, the immediate problem to be faced was that – save for Hardie, himself – the new 'Labour' grouping on the opposition benches had failed to materialise. Joseph Arch and Havelock Wilson had also been elected, alongside Keir Hardie and John Burns, but Cunninghame Graham, Ben Tillett and six more candidates who had stood for Scottish seats, had all been defeated. Moreover, contrary to expectations, John Burns – despite sitting alongside Hardie and the Parnellite MPs in the Commons – showed no interest at all in building a Labour 'party' around himself, while Arch and Havelock Wilson preferred to occupy the government benches, accepting the Liberal Party Whip as 'Lib-Lab' MPs. Relations quickly turned sour between Hardie and Burns. Their temperaments and priorities were completely different, and their egos clashed, with Burns moving ever closer to the Liberal Party machine and eventually, accepting a role within a later Liberal cabinet.[18] Hardie was, however, made of very different material and dedicated himself to creating a recognisable, independent, Labour Party, capable of fielding candidates nationwide and in its own right.

Throughout his election campaign, Hardie had emphasised bread-and-butter issues; wages, long hours, the availability and conditions of work, and standards of living. Once in Parliament, he explicitly linked the attainment of the Eight Hour Day to the question of unemployment. If working hours were cut, ran his argument, more men and women would need to be hired, thus reducing the number of those on rudimentary welfare or sunken into poverty, and bringing full employment a step nearer. In addition, with more than a nod to the old Chartist schemes of agricultural co-operatives and land companies, he advocated a form of economic self-sufficiency for the unemployed through the establishment of 'home colonies'; whereby state grants would be used to buy farm and waste land in order to found communal communities based upon exchange rather than private ownership and financial chicanery.

Unemployment was, for Hardie, the most virulent symptom of the sickness that was capitalism, and he used his maiden speech in the Commons to highlight

> all the horrors of sweating, of low wages, of long hours, and of deaths from starvation [which] are directly traceable to the

large numbers of people who are totally unemployed, or only casually employed. The worker in the workshop is fettered by the thought that outside his workshop gates there are thousands eager and willing to step into his shoes should he be dismissed in consequence of any attempt to improve his position. I therefore submit that in dealing with the problem of the unemployed we are dealing with the whole industrial problem.[19]

Keir Hardie may have had something of the aspect of a romantic and a visionary, but there was also a seam of steel folded into his being that ensured his adherence to principle, that ensured he could be neither compromised nor bought, and that he could be ruthless, when necessary, in order to achieve his goals. It was an uncomfortable combination, then as now, that did not sit well with careerist politicians or those that would always seek to extol the principles of moderation and to take the path of least resistance. Hardie would not trim, in order to secure short-term advantage, say the easy thing or act in a manner calculated to court popularity. He recognised as much himself and noted that he had the habit of saying 'the right thing in the wrong place'; and in this lay the ruin of his career as the MP for West Ham.[20]

Support Fragments

The Liberal Party in West Ham attempted to find a suitable candidate to run against him, but despite their vocal criticism of the independent – and increasingly socialist – ground he had occupied in Parliament, their energies were expended in internecine quarrels amongst themselves and, in the end, they could find no one willing, or able, to stand as their own candidate in the General Election of 1895. If the complex web of alliances that had propelled Hardie to Westminster had slowly begun to pull apart, then he made matters worse by consciously shredding his relations with the Congregationalist chapels, after telling the ministers that:

The reason why the Labour Party has turned its back on the church is because the church has turned its back on Christ... You preach to the respectability of your congregations... [but] you forget the withering and suffering masses outside the walls of your churches.[21]

At the same time, divisions in Irish nationalist politics had opened up and the repercussions of Parnell's destruction at the hands of the clerics spilled into West Ham. Keir Hardie was decried from the pulpit as both a socialist agitator – a theological crime in itself, in the wake of the First Vatican Council – and as a close supporter of Charles Stewart Parnell, the hero turned pariah. Father Timothy Ring, a local parish priest, thundered that the hatred of the Tories should not stand between his flock and 'putting Keir Hardie out' of power; the words of a young James Connolly, writing to the Irish and Catholic voters, in support of Hardie's re-election, went largely unnoticed.

Perhaps more damaging still was Hardie's record of attendance at Westminster and his apparent neglect of his own constituency, that came increasingly to be criticised within the pages of the local press. Every day spent in Parliament, and away from his careers as journalist and paid speaker, effectively reduced Hardie's income. He kept up a gruelling round of activities which may have effectively burned him out and though still a young man, the face that stares out from the photographs taken of him as MP for West Ham show him as being careworn and prematurely aged.

If Hardie's religious and Liberal support was evaporating, then he was also troubled by divisions within his own natural supporters on the left. The Fabian Society failed to formally affiliate with the ILP and locally were foundering and rudderless at a point when they could have been actively assisting with Hardie's re-election. The SDF branches, swayed no doubt by Hyndman's intense personal disdain and Engels' harsh critique of Hardie as a dilettante and show-boater, had also cooled in their enthusiasm, and Will Thorne was repeatedly urged to throw his hat in to the ring and challenge Hardie for the socialist nomination. West Ham was certainly too small a borough to contain two such large figures and though Thorne never publicly criticised Hardie and refused to split the Socialist vote, in 1895, the pair certainly clashed. Certainly, the Gasworkers' union canvassed more selectively for the Labour candidate in 1895, than it had three years earlier but remained the backbone of Keir Hardie's enduring support.

In fact, it was the combination of Hardie's self-confidence and the deterioration of registration and canvassing work since 1892 that re-sulted in his defeat. Once again, Major Banes failed to mount any sort of campaigning effort. Hardie spent much of his time away from his own constituency, in 1895 campaigning up-and-down the country for other ILP candidates, while those interest groups that he had championed most energetically over the course of his parliamentary career – namely the poverty stricken and the unemployed – were largely excluded, through the property and residential qualifications, from the ability to cast their votes at the polls. The result saw a dip in the total vote from 1892, but a marked increase in the share for Major Banes, Hardie taking 3,975 votes and his Conservative opponent 4,750.[22] It would seem that alongside a switch within a segment of the Irish Catholic vote, many erstwhile Liberals – who had stayed away from the polls at the earlier election – had preferred to reject 'a Socialist, who sometimes votes Radical in the House' in favour of 'the kind of man whom Englishmen delight to honour... as near an approach to a typical John Bull as can be found – plain and straightforward.'[23]

There was no disguising the bitterness of the blow. In its aftermath, Hardie declared that:

> By a combination as strange as was ever witnessed in the political arena, I have failed to secure re-election. Every section of the community contributed its quota to the majority by which my opponent was returned. Teetotallers worked hand in hand with publicans; some trade unionists with free labourers; Liberals with Tories, priests and professed Home Rulers with Coercionists: and all to secure the defeat of the representative of Labour.[24]

Hardie, according to an account published by one of his own partisans, was laconic, filtering out the noise and the jeering on election night and confiding that no one should lose heart, 'there's plenty of work to be done in other ways to hasten on the good time. We shall live to fight and to win another day.'[25] He certainly did not walk away from the constituency after his defeat and kept his options of a return to Westminster open, remaining as the official Labour candidate for the borough until 1899.

During his three years as MP for West Ham, his own ideas had evolved from an, at times, ill-defined sense of labourism to an unequivocal identification with socialism. Perhaps the lasting impact of this process was to be found in West Ham itself, where the unemployed had occupied the council chambers and flown the Red Flag from the town hall, in 1894, and where the first Labour controlled council in British history was elected in 1898. Writing in 1899, in the *Economic Review*, Hugh Legge thought that:

the idea of Socialism is not utterly foreign to a borough which has been in part represented in Parliament by Keir Hardie. People have been taught to associate the idea with local government.[26]

The little 'splotch of Red' created on the political map by Keir Hardie's election was now growing fast and was capable, as the *Labour Leader* noted, of clearing away the 'mocking Parliament' of the rich and the self-interested, and of replacing it with something far nobler, more egalitarian, and capable of delivering economic democracy alongside the purely political. Hardie's election had, indeed, marked a sea-change in the balance of power of the land and his contemporaries realised it. As JB Glasier perceptively notes:

he was the most scorned and hated and feared of all the working-class leaders of his day by the wealthy and privileged classes and their servitors in the Press... because instinctively they perceived in him the dread apparition of the great common people divested of their servility, their ignorance and their fear... awakened to consciousness of their rights, their power, their contempt of those who had degraded and robbed them... bidding their lords and oppressors betake themselves from their rent offices and cash rooms, from Parliament and the sovereignty of the nation! – Bidding them, in fact, be off the back of Labour for ever![27]

'Socialism is the natural faith of these people and it is catching on.'

CHAPTER 9

Merthyr Tydfil: Hardie's Welsh Odyssey

Owen Smith

THE PLOUGH TIP in Aberaman was a grassed-over hillock when I slid down it in the upturned bonnet of an old Morris Minor in 1970s South Wales, unrecognisable, to my child's eye at least, as the slag-heap residue of pits long-gone. I don't really remember either, whether it was my collier grandfather, still working then, and whose terraced house overlooked the Plough, or my historian father, who first told me that Keir Hardie once spoke to thousands from that mount. Hardie gave a hundred or more such 'Cinder Hall' sermons in the years that paved the way to his election, in 1900, as MP for the Merthyr Boroughs, and foreran Labour's emergence as the party of Wales and of the working class throughout Great Britain. Forty years after I tobogganed that tip, a century after Hardie's death, and a few months after our defeat in May 2015, it's time to summon up Keir's spirit – an endeavour he would have wholeheartedly endorsed[1] – and ask what he might tell us today about the route back to power.

But first to explain how he came to Wales, via Lanark and London, to be loved as few 'Welsh' politicians, before or since, and to connect with this community better 'than ever their own Welsh-speaking leaders had'. Hardie's political trade was learned in the pits and the union politics of the Lanarkshire coalfield. The danger and hardship of life underground, the industrial struggle for employment, pay and better conditions, a Celtic culture and a nascent Labour consciousness might all have seemed familiar in the iron and anthracite towns of south Wales, but Hardie only visited for the first time in 1887, aged 31, to address the Trades Unions Congress in Swansea, as the delegate of the Ayrshire miners.

Perhaps his fate to speak for Wales was sealed that day. Hardie used his inaugural address to launch a personal attack on the Liberal MP and TUC Chair, Henry Broadhurst, and on the TUC leadership. His charge was, in essence, that the axis of Liberal mine-owners and acquiescent Trades Unions were preventing improvements to conditions for the miners. With historian's hindsight, Henry Pelling described Hardie's intervention as the first stirring of the *New Unionism*,[2] militant and independent of the Liberal establishment. But observers at the time recalled a barrage of heckling invective, delivered in equal measure from the platform and the floor, earning infamy and opprobrium, and which his daughter, Nan, blamed for hostility to Hardie 'until the day of his death'. Either way, it got him noticed and marked the beginning of his Welsh Odyssey.

Hardie's second and most famous incursion into Welsh territory was conducted from afar, from the green benches of Westminster, where he sat as the 'Labour, Radical and Home Rule' Member for West Ham South from 1892 to 1895. His targets this time, on 28 June 1894, were fellow MPs, whom he scorned for celebrating the birth of a baby prince to the Duke and Duchess of York, without uttering a single word of condolence for the families of the 251 laid out 'stiff and stark in a Welsh valley' that very day.[3] The Albion Colliery explosion in Cilfynydd, a few miles north of Pontypridd and just south of Merthyr Tydfil, was sparked directly by greed. Impatient for greater returns, the mine-owner had quickened production with extra shifts that left no time to water the dust and damp down the blast-risk. Hardie, who as a boy of 12 had felt, first-hand, the terror of a pit disaster at the Longrigg works, could not have known the specifics of the Albion's infamous cause, but he knew its consequences all too well, and it fired his own explosion of disgust at colleagues' twin obsequiousness and indifference. The power and irreverence of Hardie's speech sparked outrage in the hall, where members 'howled and screamed', and scandalised the press outside. In Wales, however, his legend grew.

The *Labour Leader* newspaper reported the gratitude felt in South Wales Labour to

the only man with moral courage enough to protest against the mummery of congratulations in the hour of suffering and disaster.[4]

A Splendid Field

In the years, and with the approval that followed, Hardie was invited often to Wales to speak in aid of an eight-hour day, or a living wage, better health and safety or a pension in old age. However, it was in 1898, three years after he lost his West Ham seat, that Hardie became a familiar figure in person across south Wales. The minimum wage strike of that year saw Hardie crisscross the coalfields, raising funds and writing reports for the *Labour Leader*. One public meeting in Pontypridd was attended by 10,000, others in Merthyr and Dowlais, Aberdare and my grandfather's Aberaman were marched to with bands and bunting and thousands more.

Throughout, Hardie was aware he was building a following not just for himself but for the Independent Labour Party, too. Writing to its National Committee, he recorded that in south Wales 'a splendid field for ILP work was being opened up'.[5] This period cemented Hardie's reputation in South Wales as a standard bearer for the working class and laid the foundations for his electoral success in the 'Khaki' election that followed in 1900. The strike of 1898 had kindled a new spirit of political consciousness in the coalfield and disquiet, especially among miners' leaders, with their Liberal and Lib-Lab representation in Parliament. ILP branches and allied Trade Councils sprang up across the region, but it was from Merthyr, with its radical heritage, that the first call came for Hardie to stand.

Merthyr and Hardie were a match made in heaven, each with a swagger and a story to tell. Merthyr's reputation as a hotbed of radicalism had long been established. Its ironworks had been the very crucible of the Industrial Revolution. The Chartist leader, Dic Penderyn, was a Merthyr man and the memory of his martyr's death was fresh in the town's collective memory. More recently, the radical and pacifist Henry Richard had represented the Borough. Hardie's cocktail of belligerent campaigning on workers' rights and opposition to the 'Imperialist adventurism' of the Boer War found a receptive audience in the two-member constituency.

That said, it was far from certain that Hardie would win the nomination. His reputation as a trouble-maker did not sit well with some of the more conformist and conservative elements among local miners' leaders. The South Wales Miners' Federation was a hugely powerful organisation, so much so that they felt no need to affiliate yet to the TUC and no need either to hitch their heavy drams exclusively to the scrawny young pony of the ILP. Nor was it clear that Hardie could win the seat, even if nominated. The constituency was represented by two Liberal MPs, DA Thomas and Pritchard Morgan, and was expected to be strongly contested by a Tory candidate, too. Hardie certainly must have had doubts about his chances, because he hedged his bets by seeking the nomination for Preston at the same time.

In the end, he won both selections and contested the seats on consecutive days. He lost decisively in the North of England but, hot-foot to Wales, was greeted with the welcome news that the Tory candidate's poor grip of geography had seen him turn up at Newcastle-on-Tyne, thinking Merthyr somewhere nearby, and DA Thomas, a local mine-owner himself, but popular with the men, seemed sanguine about Hardie joining him on the ticket. And that is precisely what came to pass, as Hardie secured 5,745 votes, second best to Thomas, but tossing the pro-War Liberal, Pritchard Morgan, back into obscurity.

Hardie remained the MP for the Merthyr Boroughs from 1900 to his untimely death, age 59, in 1915, increasing his vote in 1906 and holding easily once more in the elections of 1910. The influence of Wales on Hardie, and on the broader labour movement throughout that tumultuous, formative period, cannot be overstated. The infamous Taff Vale judgement, which held trade unions responsible for costs to employers caused by strike action, and thus sought to break the bedrock of industrial power, was played out in the coalfields that Hardie now called home. The struggle – and victory – against Taff Vale catalysed the fusion of the ILP with the trade unions, and the birth of the modern Labour Party that followed in 1906.

Indeed, struggle was the very essence of his culture and community. The Cambrian Combine Strike of 1909–10, where my own great-grandfather was a Tonypandy rioter faced down by Churchill's troops, took place over the mountain from Hardie's Aberdare, in the neighbouring Rhondda Valleys. But Hardie, inevitably, was present to support the striking miners, to witness himself the brutality of the police and army in supressing their action, and to testify to it in Parliament and beyond.

The railwaymen's strike of the following year, the Dowlais Ironworks strike of 1912, and the sporadic strikes that took place across the coalfields throughout those years, saw Hardie, as no other labour leader of his time, connect the street to Parliament: carrying the cordite and sulphur stink of industrial conflict into the cloisters of Westminster, like smelling salts for a slumbering democracy.

Learning from Our Own Past

The relevance of these ancient conflicts to Labour's contemporary cause seems so obvious as to embarrass us with its immediacy. How, a hundred years after the Tonypandy miners rioted for a living wage, can we still be campaigning for its introduction? How can a Queen's Speech in 2015 call up the spectre of Taff Vale with its promise to curb the right to strike, and break the democratic power of our trade unions? How can we be taking backward steps on health and safety, terms and conditions in our zero-hours modernity? Perhaps Hardie would have been surprised that we still have so far to travel, and that hard won progress can be halted with such ease. But I doubt it, because he understood, as Bevan later wrote, that we can never hope to really win the struggle, just win 'changes in its terms'.[6] I think what would have surprised him, however, is modern Labour's failure to learn the lessons of our own past, some of them taught by Hardie and his generation.

First amongst those lessons is the value of our roots: in the community, in the politics of the workplace and the market square, in the culture, the concerns and the conversation of the people we represent. Hardie bridged that gap between the politics of party or parliament and the life of the community he spoke for, in word and deed. He was an activist and agitator on the streets of south Wales as well as a spokesman for socialism at home and abroad. And the one stemmed directly from the other: the power of his words was rooted in the experiences he shared with those he spoke for. As he told the audience in Merthyr's Drill Hall: 'I love the people to whom I belong – I am one of yourselves.'[7]

That word, 'love', has lessons for us, too, because Hardie's connection with his people was built on more than shared experience or a common class identity. It was about an emotional connection that went beyond any material or political self-interest which might have bound the working class to Labour. Hardie understood that Labour is a mission and movement, not merely a vehicle to win power. Power is the means. But the mission, for equality, for freedom, for fulfilment unbounded by class or birth or blood, is far bigger than the means to its achievement. And to sustain the will to seize that power, and achieve those noble ends, you need more than reason and rationale, you need the raw emotion of hope and desire, anger and ambition.

So he was mocked by the theoreticians and the calculators – the triangulators of his day – for the emotional, almost spiritual conviction of his socialism and for the absence of economic argument in much of his writing and speeches. His socialism, infused with Christianity and shaped, too, by the secular spiritualism of the time, was seen by many of his contemporaries as out of step with the cool modernism of Edwardian England. But in our own modern era, in which politics seems seldom to escape the arid territory of economic rationalism, let alone ascend to higher planes of hope for social transformation, Hardie's politics of passionate desire and gut-felt conviction, can be a light that guides Labour back to the people, and to power. Our words must inspire hope, as much as our policies inspire trust.

The actions of Hardie's ILP in Merthyr and Aberdare holds lessons for us, too. Often in London or abroad, he played little practical part himself in the development of the local Labour Party into a network of social and educational activity. But his enthusiasm for grass roots activism of almost any kind set a context for that growth. He rejected the militant syndicalism of *The Miner's Next Step*, but was buoyed by the engagement and consciousness that it fuelled. More prosaically, but surely as importantly, he rejoiced in the early development of ILP Institutes and Libraries, theatre companies and marching bands, cycling clubs and 'smokers' concerts'. The organising and management of recreation and education stitched early Labour into the warp and weft of community life, creating assets owned by the people and for the people: symbolising possibility, building local capacity and forging solidarity.

Modern Labour's rediscovery of 'community organising' and municipal socialism seems feeble next to the mighty edifices built by that earlier generation, but their inspiration should spur us on. Just as Hardie's Labour built from the grassroots, so must we, remaking Labour's reputation as the catalyst for community action and collective self-improvement. Local government can be the main route to this renaissance, but extra-institutional action through community activism, to renew things like leisure activities, or even to run core public services, must also be our focus. In towns like Pontypridd, where miners' pennies built our park, the modern equivalent of community self-help is emerging in the transfer of assets – theatres or libraries – from the council to the community. Though the cause may be Tory cutbacks, the outcomes can spark Labour's fightback.

Building a Base

Most important of all the lessons Hardie might teach Labour in 2015 is the simple nostrum that though our ends need not change, the means surely must. The fluidity of the Labour politics that Hardie knew, with competing factions and forces, and no certainty that our party would emerge as dominant, has obvious overtones for our age. Hardie's conception of Labour was as a party of the working class, with the clear objective of achieving equality through socialism. But he was a pragmatist and an opportunist, too, alive to the possibility of advancing his cause through other routes, with other partners, and of exploiting events and ideas with agility and élan. His engagement with the women's movement, his alliances of convenience with syndicalists, communists or Welsh nationalists all testify to what Ken O Morgan calls 'his ethic [of] the broad church, gradualist, tolerant, solid, subordinating doctrinal divisions to practical action on behalf of specific objectives'.[8]

In that sense he was a model for other successful Labour leaders, able to adapt swim with the currents of their age, without losing sight of the higher ground we must always be striving for.

In this context, and in light of our present debate about the future of Labour and of the union of Great Britain, Hardie's ambivalent attitude to nationalism is worthy of some scrutiny. Often described, by himself and others as a Home Ruler, Hardie's sense of national identity was necessarily complex. A Scotsman and an internationalist, representing a Welsh seat in London, his faith in Home Rule appeared, in part, to be inspired by his faith that the Welsh, like the Scots, were socialists by birth. In *Socialism and the Celt* (1907), he writes:

All Celtic people are, at heart, communists... All the qualities for which the people of Wales are most famous and on which they pride themselves most are... those which have come down from their communistic forefathers. The qualities which are in the blood and which will keep asserting themselves, are they not part of the race as much as the features of the language? And the love of socialism is one of the strongest of these.

Perhaps the traditional support of the Welsh people for Labour bears testimony to a truth in Hardie's words, but, if so, the mass transit of loyalties in Scotland begs more profound questions about its sustainability. In any event, Hardie's attraction to the concept of Home Rule was in reality born less of his faith in a genetic predisposition to socialism, more in his belief in local action and accountability as the vital foundations for his political party and project. As he told his followers in Merthyr: 'It is as a Socialist, a Trade Unionist and social reformer that I base my chief claim to your support.'[9] Home Rule, then, was more a means of galvanising men and women to action, of harnessing the energy of their national identity to the cause of social and economic reform for all nations. As his contemporary, John Littlejohns writes: 'Socialism is the end, Home Rule the means.'[10]

That simple sentence may best explain how Hardie imagined the Red Dragon could be stitched onto the Red Flag of socialism. And its confident simplicity might also help us understand how we should now respond to the loss of allegiance to our party in Scotland and the fight we face in Wales, too. Labour delivered devolution to Wales and Scotland, but the truth is that we have never fully embraced it. The view of the devolved administrations from the centre, both Whitehall and Westminster, has been a mixture of grudging acceptance, snooty condescension and wilful ignorance, while the reverse view has often been chippy resentfulness at achievements unacknowledged and self-determination unfulfilled.

Yet more profound than any superficial scratchiness in relationships between the new and old institutions of government, is the fundamental challenge that devolution always presented to the logic of Labour. Labour's raison d'etre is equality and social justice and the means to achieving those goals has been central control over the levers of taxation and redistribution. Administrative devolution, decentralised decisions about how to spend central allocations, could always logically reconcile with that framework. But national identity, the pride and passion of belonging, is not logical, it is emotional at base, and the framework we built was never going to contain it.

So we asserted from the centre that the rational thing to do was to stick together. We pointed out the facts that the tax base in the north and west of Britain is subsidised by the south. We appealed to the heads of those who can surely see we are stronger united. And in so doing, we filled the hearts of those we addressed with resentment and detachment from our party. Scotland left us, and we didn't even see them packing their bags.

And yet the very scale of our defeat expands the opportunity to rebuild. This time our foundations must stand on the type of emotional connection Hardie tapped into, as much as on the economic self-interest of shared risk. That will require a fundamental reassessment of how Labour can achieve our mission of equality within a looser union. It may demand new party structures and coalition-building both within and beyond our party. It may also mean that we accept variance in tax rates and benefits across the UK. But these looser bonds cannot be allowed to mean lesser equality, so Labour will need to renew our vow to see every nation and region, every family and community, thrive and prosper, even if the means to those ends are more diffuse and distributed than in the past. And we will need to work harder, and figure out new ways to stop wealth and opportunity from pooling in London and the south. Home rule can still be the means, but social justice must remain our end.

Hardie would have got that. And got on with it, too. His trajectory, from Liberalism to Labour, from pit to Parliament and through every nation of these isles, was an arc of adaptation to circumstance, but unerring in its aim. He teaches us that we can remain flexible in our route to power; that our politics can accommodate and affiliate without losing potency, provided we retain a clear sense of what we are for – a more equal society and a just economy. Socialism, as we still might call it. When Hardie first came to Wales, the authors of the *South Wales Labour Annual* were moved to write: 'The presence of Keir Hardie in our midst is working wonders.' Let's make sure his memory can do the same.

'I am not specially anxious to go to Parliament, but I am anxious and determined that the wants and wishes of the working classes shall be made known and attended to there.'

CHAPTER 10

Cumnock: A Lasting Legacy

Cathy Jamieson

FOR ANYONE INVOLVED with the Labour Party the importance of James Keir Hardie cannot be overstated. As the founding father of the party, he has been an inspiration over the years. In our current political climate, with Labour in opposition in the UK Parliament and the Scottish Labour Party soul-searching and seeking to redefine its relevance as a political force, it is timely to rediscover what motivated Hardie, what he stood for and how his values offer a positive vision for the future.

Although he was born and lived in Scotland, and advocated Home Rule, Keir Hardie never saw this as an end in itself. His expansive, internationalist vision transcended borders, seeing him elected as MP for English and Welsh constituencies, and led him to undertake a tour of socialist and trade union movements across Europe, attending the Second Workers' International in Paris in 1889 and the Miners' International in Belgium in 1891.

Yet wherever he travelled throughout his life, Cumnock in Ayrshire was very much his home – the place where his family was raised, and to which he returned to re-energise and refresh his thoughts.

Having myself been born and brought up in Ayrshire, and privileged to serve as an Ayrshire MSP and MP, I have a passionate interest in Keir Hardie's life in my local area.

Visitors to Cumnock can't miss the connection with Keir Hardie. Signs at the town's gateway proudly proclaim it as his home. *Lochnorris*, the house where he lived, now home to a local family, is marked simply by a small plaque on the wall. A short walk away stands the church where he was a member. A further short walk leads to the Baird Institute, where a permanent exhibition marks his life and work, with many of his possessions on display.

In the town hall, the bronze bust of Hardie by sculptor Benno Schotz stands in prime position, making it a popular spot for photo calls for aspiring politicians and for many of the 'Keirs' of today to take 'selfies'.

Nearby Keir Hardie Hill is one of several streets in Ayrshire to be named after him. And just up the hill from the town hall, in Cumnock cemetery, a marble headstone marks where his ashes are interred.

But it's not just these physical reminders which mark his legacy locally. He is very much alive in the hearts of local people.

During my first election campaign in Cumnock in 1999, I was engaged in what might best be described as a lively conversation with two young men – both of whom were experiencing difficulties in their lives – but who broke off their own argument to talk to me about what they believed Keir Hardie would have thought of the new Scottish Parliament.

On a recent visit to the Baird Institute with Richard Leonard of the Keir Hardie Society, I met two local school pupils who had been studying Hardie's life and works. They were excited by the local connection and that the Society had been set up to keep his memory and values alive. Keen to learn as much as possible, they were volunteering at the Baird Institute.

And campaigning locally, I didn't need to ask any questions of one pensioner, who simply pointed to the window of his home, in which was proudly displayed a miniature plaster bust of Keir Hardie, made by the late Bill Dick, a local artist and member of the Keir Hardie Society.

Keir Hardie's daughter Nan, who was brought up in *Lochnorris*, is also remembered for her own role in local politics, as a councillor and provost. She married Emrys Hughes, who went on to become MP for South Ayrshire, and also wrote a biography of Hardie.

A Lasting Legacy

To understand Keir Hardie's legacy, it is useful to look back at his life in Cumnock, at what brought him there and his roles in the trade union movement and local community.

James Keir Hardie and his wife Lillie arrived in Cumnock in 1879, to organise the local miners. Still only in his early 20s, he nonetheless brought with him organising experience, having already been the Corresponding Secretary of Lanarkshire miners and a delegate to a National Conference of Miners held in Glasgow. He had been the local Miners Agent, and during a six-week strike in Lanarkshire, he helped to run a food kitchen for striking miners' families, persuading local merchants to provide the supplies on the promise that they would be paid in due course.

Interestingly, Hardie was not the first to attempt to organise the Ayrshire miners. The first union amongst Scottish miners after the repeal of the Combination Laws was founded by colliers from 27 pits around Kilmarnock, who met on 25 October 1824.

The *Kilmarnock Address* set out the formation of a trade union of mineworkers, known as the Colliers' Association and demanded that limits be placed on the powers and privileges of the coal-masters. Following the repeal of the Combination Acts, which had outlawed trade union organisation, they wanted to stabilise wages, end the practice of employers bringing in more compliant labour to undercut the miners, and provide strike pay to members. The document emphasised the need for collective self-reliance, and the need for miners themselves to provide for the dependants of those injured or killed. Later that year, some 1,400 Ayrshire miners were on strike for over two months. Although the Colliers' Association seems to have disappeared after that, the need for such an organisation was as great as ever when Keir Hardie answered the call to come to Ayrshire.

In August 1881 the newly formed Ayrshire Miners' Association put forward a demand for a 10 per cent increase in wages. Unsurprisingly, this was promptly rejected by the mine owners. Despite a lack of funds for strike pay, a strike was called. Although this action ended in the miners returning to work after ten weeks without their demands being met, not long afterwards wages were raised across the board by the mine owners, apparently fearful of future action.

There were consequences for Hardie personally, as the miners could no longer afford to pay him and he lost his job.

By chance, an opportunity arose to begin writing for the local newspaper when the minister of the Evangelical Union to which Hardie belonged fell ill. The minister had been a contributor to the *Cumnock News* and Hardie took over his weekly column. This helped make ends meet and he made the most of this opportunity.

The *Cumnock News* was an offshoot of the *Ardrossan and Saltcoats Herald*, owned and edited by Arthur Guthrie, a staunch Liberal who was prepared to stand up against the powerful local land and coal owning interests.

Hardie titled his weekly feature 'Black Diamonds' and signed it 'The Trapper' – a reference to his former job regulating the flow of air in a dark Lanarkshire mine, with only rats and ponies for company.

In his columns he promoted self-reliance, temperance and thrift. But he also exposed lack of safety in the pits and the racketeering of company stores. He attacked charges for supposedly free education and championed the extension of the franchise and votes for women. He also wrote on international issues, denouncing jingoism and the slaughter of 'Arabs fighting for home and liberty'.

His continued efforts to organise the miners saw the formation of the Ayrshire Miners' Union in August 1886. Writing in his biography of Keir Hardie, William Stewart refers to the founding meeting:

> The exact date is not known nor the place of nativity, early records having apparently been lost. James Neil, of Cumnock, who took an active part in the early work of the Union, has recollections of a delegate meeting in Mauchline, at which Andrew Fisher, of Crosshouse, (afterwards Prime Minister of Australia) was present, and he thinks this may have been the initial meeting, which is not unlikely, Fisher, like Neil himself, being one of the original delegates.[1]

However it began, Hardie became the Organising Secretary of the new union, drawing a modest salary of £75 per year – equivalent to around £8,700 today.

The following year, in 1887, Hardie launched a monthly journal, *The Miner*. While he started the paper mainly to highlight miners' problems and grievances, like his newspaper column, it became a vehicle for him to express his own views on a range of issues. Speaking at meetings and gatherings in the coalfields also gave him a platform to promote his belief that working people could not and should not rely on others to free them from the problems they faced in their everyday lives.

He argued that poverty was far from inevitable, and that just as it was a result of man-made conditions, so too could those conditions be re-made differently. He argued vehemently that unfair conditions were not something to be endured, but had to be abolished.

A Socialist

It was in Cumnock that Keir Hardie formed his ideas and political philosophy. Many of his later speeches and writings were composed at *Lochnorris*. The property was built in 1891, using capital loaned by Adam Birkmyre, who admired Hardie's work. In an original letter, recently given to the Keir Hardie Society for safe keeping, Hardie advises the District Valuer's office in Ayr that he had bought the site in 1890 for £100, and that the value of the property was £1,250.

While Keir Hardie's values and principles were undoubtedly set in his early years from personal experience of hard times, they were undoubtedly shaped further by the first few years of his time in Cumnock. The struggle of the miners he represented was fundamental to his work and his emerging political beliefs. When the Scottish Miners' Federation was formed in 1887, Hardie was appointed its Secretary.

In addition to his writing, Keir Hardie continued to be actively involved in the local community. He was active in the Good Templar Lodge and church work and it is said that he preached from the pulpit on occasions in the minister's absence, as well as on street corners in Cumnock and neighbouring villages. He set up an evening class two nights a week, passing on his own self-taught shorthand skills – further evidence of his commitment to being involved at all levels to make change in society, and to help others gain skills.

During this period of his life, Keir Hardie was developing his thinking on the wider political scene, and coming to the conclusion that the Liberal Party was not going to deliver the changes that the working class needed.

In his capacity as Secretary of the Ayrshire Miners' Union, Keir Hardie took forward his vision of an alternative. In May, 1887, Ayrshire miners held demonstrations on Irvine Moor and on Craigie Hill, and adopted the following resolution:

> That in the opinion of this meeting, the time has come for the formation of a Labour Party in the House of Commons, and we hereby agree to assist in returning one or more members to represent the miners of Scotland at the first available opportunity.[2]

Shortly afterwards Hardie was adopted as the miners' candidate. In October of that year Hardie made clear that it was time for people to make their choice about who they wanted to go forward to represent them.

> The Liberals and Conservatives have, through their organisations, selected candidates. They are both, as far as I know, good men. The point I wish to emphasise, however, is this: that these men have been selected without the mass of the people being consulted. Your betters have chosen the men, and they now send them down to you to have them returned. What would you think if the Miners' Executive Council were to meet in Kilmarnock and appoint a secretary to the miners of Ayrshire in that way? Your candidate ought to be selected by the voice and vote of the mass of the people.

In putting forward this view, Hardie was clear that it was not good enough for a small committee of Liberal bigwigs to decide the candidate of working people. He wanted an organised membership, drawn from local communities, to be involved in candidate selection, and emphasised that he was not seeking a parliamentary position for his own ends, but for the cause of working-class people:

> I will endeavour to have a Labour Electoral Association formed in every town and village in the constituency... I am not specially anxious to go to Parliament, but I am anxious and determined that the wants and wishes of the working classes shall be made known and attended to there.[3]

Keir Hardie's onward journey did of course take him to Parliament when, after defeat in the Mid Lanark by-election in 1888, he subsequently became MP for West Ham, and later for Merthyr Tydfil.

He has been described as Labour's 'greatest strategist, prophet and evangelist'. In his own terms, he was first and foremost a socialist:

> I am a Socialist, and until industry is organised on a co-operative basis, wherein men shall work, not to make profit, but to produce the necessaries of life for the community, the evils complained of will never be eradicated. But much might be done by providing work for the unemployed on home colonies, where those out of work could provide for themselves the necessaries of life. A minimum wage might also with advantage – especially to

working girls – be established, making it a penal offence for an employer to engage a worker under a sum sufficient to ensure the necessaries of life. A restriction of the hours of labour to eight per day, or less, in dangerous and unhealthy occupations; a drastic reform of the land laws which would stop or tend to minimise at least the influx of the agricultural labourers to the town; the prohibition of work in dwelling-houses, and the erection of workshops by the municipality wherein work now performed at home could be undertaken, these having crèches attached for the benefit of women with children called upon to earn a living for themselves; and the establishment by the State of provision for the disabled, whether by old age, sickness, or accident – all these would tend to check the deterioration now going on, and give the workers an opportunity to work out their industrial freedom on the lines which experience will suggest as being the best. The municipalities should provide homes which would conform in every particular to sanitary laws, and provide such appliances as are deemed absolutely necessary in middle-class houses, so that the people, and especially the working women, would be able to maintain a sense of cleanliness, which is utterly impossible today, Recreation-rooms and reading-rooms should be abundantly provided, especially in poor quarters, together with small open spaces laid down in grass for children to play upon, and thus preserve their contact with nature and mother earth, the loss of which is accountable for much of the atheism which is a natural product of city life.[4]

In Parliament he fervently supported the rights of women, a principled and, by the standards of the time, highly progressive stance which brought him into constant conflict with many. He was a pacifist who exposed himself to intense criticism by opposing the First World War; and an internationalist and citizen of the world, who preached fraternity and solidarity across nations, and fiercely descried the cruelty, avarice, and will to dominate exhibited by the ruling elite, both at home and abroad.

His was the founding ideology on which the Independent Labour Party was predicated and his values and vision provided many of the key precepts and pillars of 20th century and, indeed, modern socialism: working-class solidarity; equal rights (for women as well as men); the redistribution of wealth and resources; the need for care and compassion towards the jobless, the voiceless, and those bereft of hope.

Looking back at the report he presented to the Scottish Miners' Federation in 1887, his manifesto was straightforward – people before profit, a co-operative approach to industry, work for the jobless, minimum wage, healthier and safer working conditions, child care, decent homes, State provision for the elderly, disabled and the sick, access to education and leisure facilities, open spaces and land reform. All of these are issues which have relevance in today's world.

Keir Hardie's vision and values were born from his working-class upbringing and his trade union activity. He would expect the present day Labour Party to put the interests of working people first. He would not understand the calls – on either side – for the Labour Party and the Trade Unions to go separate ways, and would expect the whole Labour movement to work in co-operation to protect the interests of working people, locally, nationally and internationally.

Keeping his legacy alive doesn't mean living in the past. His fundamental values and principles must be translated into a modern day context. The demand for a Living Wage, an end to zero hours contracts, prosecution of those who flout health and safety laws, the right to strike, the protection of human rights and tackling inequality are all live issues today worthy of campaigns in his name.

As an advocate of Home Rule, he would approve of a Scottish Parliament, but would surely expect it to be serving the interests of the working class rather than becoming an end in itself. Improving educational attainment for all, tackling the public health issues of today, building affordable homes and provision of leisure facilities for all to use, creating communities where people feel safe would surely be amongst his priorities for the Scottish Parliament to deliver on.

For a Better Life

Keir Hardie was a tough man, born at a tough time and into a tough and unforgiving world. That toughness and the resilience it afforded him was an essential, integral part of his character. But he never allowed his own toughness and experience of suffering to inure him to the suffering of others. Nor did he come to regard his own personal achievements as evidence that anyone can pull themselves up by their bootstraps. Having made his own way in the world, he sought, first and foremost, to ensure that others had the opportunity to do likewise.

He was born amid the people, died a man of the people, and fought with every breath to give the people a better life. In a world where politics, and politicians, are variously descried as 'corrupt', 'venal' and 'in it for themselves', where ideology is seen as expendable, the price one pays for power, Hardie's resistance to the trappings of prestige and privilege are nothing short of remarkable.

He never forgot the people he was proud to represent, and the cause of the miners had a special place in his heart. In October 1910, he wrote from *Lochnorris* to Mr Andrew Sharp, JP, Miners Agent in Maryport, enclosing a bank draft for £50 which he had received from the Illawarra Colliery Employees' Association, Woonona, New South Wales, to be used for immediate relief for widows and relatives of the disaster at Wellington Colliery. He added his own thoughts to the letter:

> It is most touching to find how the terrible calamity has drawn out the sympathy of these miners away on the other side of the globe, and I am certain should the occasion ever arise, which I pray it may not, we on this side would not be slow in imitating their fine example.

Always an internationalist, it was, sadly, international events which saw Hardie die a broken man, reviled by many for his opposition to one of the greatest human catastrophes of the 20th century – the First World War. He opposed the war because he understood that it was nothing more than a colonial power play and was devastated by both the loss of so many young lives and the failure of the working classes to work together in the common pursuit of peace.

Yet if Hardie regretted the manner of his ending, he would not have altered it, because he lived not for popularity, but for principles.

Perhaps that is the most powerful message to be taken from his life's work, and the real legacy for the Labour Party.

*'My work has consisted of trying to
stir up a divine discontent with wrong'*

CHAPTER II

An Agitator: The Enduring Principle of Agitation

Melissa Benn

TIMING IS ALL, and nowhere more so than in politics. When Keir Hardie died in September 1915, just over a year after the onset of the First World War, 'his life was widely regarded a failure' – in part, perhaps, because of his brave and lonely stand against that very war.[1] Bob Holman describes how at Hardie's funeral

> nobody represented the House of Commons [but] multitudes of working-class men and women lined the streets. [Hardie] died believing that most of the objectives he had campaigned for were lost.'[2]

Subsequent judgements of Hardie have been more discerning and justly appreciative. This, after all, was the man who, in the words of one Hardie biographer, Kenneth O Morgan, 'rose from the pits of Ayrshire to change the world': a founder and leader of the Labour Party, a tireless and prominent labour movement journalist and editor, and a major figure on the international socialist stage.[3]

But if Hardie's life remains exemplary today, it is largely because he embodied one of the enduring laws of politics: that it is largely popular pressure that brings about change, and the litmus test of a democracy is how well it absorbs and responds to movements beyond established institutions. Hardie had no love for Westminster and its arcane and self-satisfied rituals, but, rejecting the route of violent revolution, he recognised the need for the representation of radical ideas within Parliament, and the embodiment of just demands in law and policy. In his view, Labour needed to 'capture power, not destroy it'.[4]

For Hardie, then, the key to politics lay in what he often called 'agitation': principled, powerful, often unruly, popular protest. Throughout his remarkable but relatively short life (he died at 59) he demonstrated an unstinting commitment to the rebellions and restlessness of those excluded from power or used agitation himself to promote often unpopular causes. Agitation was at the heart of three of the most significant movements of his lifetime – the representation of labour, the struggle for women's suffrage and pacifism.

The son of a domestic servant and a carpenter, Hardie came from the Scottish working class and the experiences of his early life, including a period working as a 'trapper' and a pony driver in the mines, 'scarred the very springs of [his] being' and made him 'frantic' to do something to alleviate the misery of others.[5] Self-educated, articulate, sympathetic and apparently fearless, he was an effective union organiser from a young age and for a large part of his parliamentary life represented Merthy Tydfil, a strong mining constituency in Wales.

A Socialist, Not a Statist

From the 1880s onwards, Hardie became a distinctive voice in labour movement politics on the Scottish and then the national stage. The Lanarkshire miners' strike in the winter of 1887 and the silence of the Liberal press in response to police brutality 'abruptly changed the key of Hardie's activity'.[6] Hardie urged the men to 'make their power felt'. He was also prescient enough to understand the significance, and welcome the rise, of the movement to organise unskilled workers, the so-called new unionism of the 1880s. Hardie's radicalism put him on a collision course with union officialdom and the laissez faire individualism of the Liberal Party, at that point considered the parliamentary representative of trade unionism. But Hardie 'won the day' and in 1890 he persuaded the TUC, for the first time, to support an eight-hour day.

As David Miliband argued in 2010, when himself contesting the Labour leadership:

> Hardie's greatest act of political strategy was to reject incorporation into the Liberal Party and seek an independent movement, based upon its own values and practices, and pursuing a common good... Hardie said, repeatedly, that although there were many things that we can agree on with liberals, when it came to the conflict between capital and labour, between the banks and the

real economy, they would always side with the Conservatives.[7]

Hardie, Miliband was keen to stress, was a socialist, not a statist. He also rejected violent revolution, although he did talk about the 'overthrow' of the capitalist system. This contradiction was perhaps resolved not intellectually but instinctively, through his enduring advocacy of 'agitation' and his understanding of his own unique role in supporting and encouraging it. 'I am an agitator. My work has consisted of trying to stir up a divine discontent with wrong...' And again, 'The agitator who has the touch of the seer in him is a far more valuable asset than the politician. Both are necessary, but if one must be sacrificed let it not be the agitator.'[8]

Responding to 'divine discontent' put Hardie in the advance guard when it came to votes for women. Few would imagine it now, but there was, in the early 20th century, a broad, and occasionally bizarre, array of responses among socialists to women's suffrage, ranging from outright opposition to the principle itself to support for universal suffrage or nothing. This last position set many socialists against suffragette campaigns to extend the (then) narrower, property-based suffrage to women. Hardie 'defended... [the] limited franchise because it posed suffrage equality directly – on the single issue of gender. He also believed it had more agitational potential and... would draw more women into the cause and this in turn would put more pressure on Parliament to act'.[9]

Woman, the Great Unknown

Hardie was always willing to support the suffragettes, despite their violent tactics, which were controversial in both conservative and labour movement circles, and even after Emmeline and Christabel Pankhurst, the leaders of the suffragette organisation the Women's Social and Political Union (WPSU) publicly rejected him. Hardie could be guaranteed to draw, or massively augment, large crowds at suffragette meetings, and he always spoke up for the WPSU in Parliament, particularly on the issue of force feeding. He became very close to Sylvia Pankhurst, whose social vision was far broader than that of her sister and mother, who moved eventually towards the Conservative Party, but most thought it was the powerful Emmeline who exercised the greater hold over Hardie. Certainly, it was the only time in his life he put any other interest above a pure class interest.

Later, he would claim that 'woman, even more than the working class, is the great unknown'.[10] He grasped how the notorious 'double shift' for women crippled their life chances: 'I saw that if the boy went out to work – in effect, he could play or study in the evening, but whatever a woman did, she had another lot of work to do when she got home. This was grossly unfair…'[11]

Unlike his fellow Labour MP George Lansbury, another fierce supporter of women's rights, Hardie's understanding did not always extend to his own household. Hardie's wife Lillie and daughter Nan were fiercely loyal to him, but the punishing nature of his political work meant he spent little time with them, and his fame and notoriety was more psychologically imprisoning to them than to Hardie himself. As women, and particularly as women without any public or professional role, they lacked the sense of agency afforded to those who are directly involved in struggle or public work. It can be far worse to experience harsh criticism of a loved one, with no chance to respond. Both women suffered continual ill health that would today probably be categorised as depression or anxiety. Theirs was a very different, more highly personal form, of agitation.

'The Price of the Ticket'

Taking up, and holding to, an unpopular political stand requires exceptional qualities that few are born with or ever manage to acquire. In 1894, after an explosion in a Pontypridd mine which killed 251 men, Hardie requested in Parliament that a message of condolence to the relatives of the victims be added to an address of congratulations on the birth of a royal heir, the future Edward VIII. The request was refused and Hardie made a speech attacking the servility that surrounds a monarchy supported by the tax payer. In his book on royalty, Jeremy Paxman records both Hardie's speech and the viscerally hostile response he provoked from fellow MPs:

> From his childhood onward this boy will be surrounded by sycophants and flatterers by the score – [Cries of 'Oh, oh!'] – and will be taught to believe himself as of a superior creation. [Cries of 'Oh, oh']. A line will be drawn between him and the people whom he is to be called upon someday to reign over. In

due course, following the precedent which has already been set, he will be sent on a tour round the world, and probably rumours of a morganatic alliance will follow – [Loud cries of 'Oh, oh!' and 'Order!'] – and the end of it all will be that the country will be called upon to pay the bill. [Cries of 'Divide!'].[12]

According to a contemporary observer, 'The House rose at him like a pack of wild dogs. His voice was drowned in a din of insults and the drumming of feet on the floor. But he stood there, white-faced, blazing-eyed, his lips moving, though the words were swept away.' Unsurprisingly, the newspapers savagely attacked Hardie for his speech.[13]

Hardie's militant pacifism put him at the receiving end of a very different kind of agitation and was, almost certainly, the most unpopular cause that he ever championed. When he opposed the Boer War (1899–1902) the offices of the *Labour Leader*, the paper he edited, were attacked and organised pro-war mobs would regularly invade, and disrupt, his public meetings. Despite this, Hardie toured the country tirelessly putting the case against this 'foul crime'.

Many believe that Hardie's outspoken opposition to the First World War in 1914 finally broke him. When he put the case against the war, jingoists prevented him speaking, even in his own constituency of Merthyr Tydfil. His future son-in-law Emrys Hughes describes how Hardie was pursued by a 'howling mob. He looked neither left nor right, his head erect, grey-haired, grey-bearded chieftain, one of the grandest men that had ever braved the rabble.'[14]

Ten days later he warned his daughter off from accompanying him to the station in their home town of Cumnock because he did not want her to experience the insults that were likely to be hurled at him. One biographer, Caroline Benn, says that 'Hardie was abused in print and in public as never before...'[15]

Hardie's near contemporary, Ramsay MacDonald, who also stood out against the war, vowed to himself that he would never face such opprobrium again, so personally unbearable did he find it. But for Hardie, vilification was the 'price of the ticket'. His courage made him formidable but the personal price was high. His friends and contemporaries believed that the public onslaught that he faced as a result of his pacifism after 1914, compounded by his deep disappointment at the Labour Party's official support for the war, precipitated his stroke and then his death in the early autumn of 1915.

Struggle

Every political leader is surely drawn towards political strategies and plans that suit his or her own natural leanings or temperament. Ramsay MacDonald loved the intrigue and deal-making of politics; he was drawn to power and the social elite. Hardie was not interested in the grand or the wealthy. He saw being in Parliament as a job – and often an uncomfortable one – of representation. According to many who knew him, he had an unvarnished sympathy for human struggle and difficulty, and an innate sense of fairness. He was also kind, that precious human quality which the writer Jan Morris has called 'the ruling principle of nowhere'. Isabella Ford, a prominent member of the National Union of Women's Suffrage Societies, a more moderate and broad-based organisation than the WPSU, said of Hardie:

> His extraordinary sympathy with the women's movement, his complete understanding of what it stands for, were what first made me understand the finest side of his character. In the days when labour men neglected and slighted the women's cause or ridiculed it, Hardie never once failed us, never once faltered in his work for us. We women can never forget what we owe him.[16]

Hardie felt at ease among working people and the politically passionate, those excluded from power and Parliament. For him, agitation – the crowd, the huge public meeting, the vast demonstration – represented not a threat but the liberation of mass energies, the promise of new possibilities. He was a gifted public speaker who felt at home on a platform. Such 'outdoor' work, as he sometimes called it, was his natural calling. He loved to travel, particularly at times when domestic politics was tricky, and he could almost always be guaranteed huge and enthusiastic audiences abroad, where he was often treated as a greater hero than he was at home. Hardie regularly spoke to audiences of thousands around the world.

By contrast, he found Parliament a deeply uncongenial place and the more nuanced, diplomatic or compromising aspects of parliamentary leadership, repugnant. It was generally agreed that he did not perform well as the Labour Party's first leader in Parliament. Hardie's skill was in building the various institutions that went into the making of the modern Labour Party (officially formed in 1906) – from the trades unions to the Independent Labour Party to the Labour Representation Committee. For him, the main aim of the Labour Party in Parliament was to enact laws that would protect the hard-working poor and those who were unemployed through no fault of their own, and to extend the rights of citizens; so he championed a limited working day, proper health and safety measures, a free education, universal health care and fair pensions. Hardie's political tenacity and integrity as well as his basic programme for a decent life for every citizen was surely an important part of the legacy drawn upon by the post-war Labour Government that so famously established the modern welfare state.

The Gains

What would Hardie have made of politics, and the Labour Party, of the modern age? We can be absolutely certain that he would have opposed the Iraq war. He would have grasped the slippery politics of coalition more easily than a later generation of Labour leaders, for as David Miliband said soon after the formation of the Coalition government in 2010, 'In some ways we are back to Hardie's time, where the Conservative and Liberal Parties wish to exclude Labour from power.'[17] As for the SNP, Hardie might well have cheered the example of a strong, working-class woman from Ayrshire heading up a significant block of radical MPs at Westminster, but his own support for Scottish Home Rule stopped far short of nationalism.

He would, surely, have been amazed at those very achievements of the post-war Labour government that are now in the process of being dismantled or are under threat: universal free education, a publicly funded and run National Health Service, state pensions and child benefit. In some ways, he would have been familiar with the rising inequality of our own time, with the growth of food banks, zero hour contracts, continuing unemployment, low wages and lack of adequate housing. He would surely have championed the living wage and been one of the lone, brave voices against the current cross party austerity agenda, making the case for investment in the creation of well paid jobs in those areas ravaged by deindustrialisation, now so vulnerable to UKIP.

A political animal like Hardie would have instinctively supported the multiple 'agitations' of our own time from the Occupy movements of 2011–12 to the rise of fourth wave feminism (although he'd have had quite a bit of catching up to do on the 'women front') to the New Era and Focus E15 campaigns to prevent evictions and the 'social cleansing' of benefit claimants. In these conformist times, his uncompromising republicanism would (still) have got him into trouble. Few Labour MPs would today dare make such anti-monarchist speech as Hardie made in 1894, nor risk the predictable avalanche of abuse from the press, which has become even more hostile and intrusive over the past century.

Portraits of Hardie, with his soulful, prematurely aged, face and full beard, appear to speak to us of a vanished age. It would be a mistake to think so. A week may be a long time in politics but a century is surprisingly short. Hardie's strong moral voice still speaks, in a variety of tongues, in today's world and exercises a powerful influence on the party that he helped set up. Ed Miliband was surely echoing him when he argued, during the 2015 election campaign, that it is popular pressure, not powerful individuals, that brings about political change. Here was a restatement, albeit in soft focus, Russell-Brand-friendly form, of the importance of that 'divine discontent', of the link between social unrest and parliamentary process. Whoever now leads the Labour Party, Keir Hardie's life teaches us that the agitation of the people always requires close, respectful attention and that just causes endure, and may eventually flourish, whatever the politicians say or do.

'I believe all the horrors of sweating, of low wages, of long hours, and of deaths from starvation, are directly traceable to the large numbers of people who are totally unemployed or only casually employed.'

Appendix 1

Keir Hardie's maiden speech to the House of
Commons, 7 February 1893

Editor's Note

THE COMMENTS ABOUT immigrants made by Keir Hardie in his maiden speech to the House of Commons must not be ignored. They are offensive in a way that is shocking. In his early days as a trade union activist he was also disparaging about Irish workers who were being brought to Lanarkshire pits to break strikes, and in his maiden speech he refers to the immigrants who would replace 'the best part of our working class'. In later years he did challenge the racism of the trade unionists he met in South Africa, arguing that they should have a 'more non-racial perspective'.[1] As a result he was run out of Pretoria by a mob of 3,000 white workers. His work with the International Socialist Bureau before the First World War brought him into contact with European socialists such as Karl Kautsky and Jean Jaurès, who both strongly condemned anti-Semitism.

KEIR HARDIE'S MAIDEN SPEECH to the House of Commons on 7 February 1893 was made in response to the following Adjournment Debate Motion:

That an humble Address be presented to Her Majesty, as followeth:–

Most Gracious Sovereign,

We, Your Majesty's most dutiful and loyal Subjects, the Commons of the United Kingdom of Great Britain and Ireland in Parliament assembled, beg leave to thank Your Majesty for the Most Gracious Speech which Your Majesty has addressed to both Houses of Parliament. – (Mr Lambert)

MR J KEIR HARDIE (WEST HAM, S)

Mr Speaker, I rise to move as an Amendment to the Address, at end, to add –

And, further, we humbly desire to express our regret that Your Majesty has not been advised when dealing with agricultural depression to refer also to the industrial depression now prevailing, and the widespread misery, due to large numbers of the working class being unable to find employment, and direct Parliament to legislate promptly and effectively in the interests of the unemployed.

It is a remarkable fact that the Speech of Her Majesty should refer to one section of industrial distress and leave the other altogether unnoticed, and there are some of us who think that if the interests of the landlords were not bound up so closely with the agricultural depression, the reference even to the agricultural labourers would not have appeared in the Queen's Speech.

The proposal which I submit to the House is not one of those referred to by the Rt Hon. Gentleman the Leader of the Government as having 'neither point nor issue', and it is my intention to take the sense of the House upon it. The question of the unemployed is to me of such importance that I would be unfaithful and untrue to every election promise I made if I did not insist on it receiving due consideration at the hands of any Government which may be in Office. As to the extent of the evil which passes under the term 'the unemployed', the monthly statements issued by the Labour Department of the Board of

Trade – based on the returns made by the leading Trade Unions of the country – show that in those trades making returns 10 per cent of their members are in receipt of out-of-work pay. That means that 10 per cent of the well-to-do artisan class, who are members of their trades unions, are unable to find employment because of the depression in trade. If we take the number of industrial workers, as it is usually taken, at 13,000,000, it will be seen that this 10 per cent means 1,300,000, when applied to the workers generally; but we have to remember that behind the workers are their wives and children and others dependent upon them.

Professor Marshall, who is a Member of the Royal Commission on Labour, stated inferentially the other day that 10 per cent of the population of the Country might be reckoned as the surplus population. That is to say, that for 10 per cent of the population no provision is made to enable them to earn for themselves and those dependent upon them the necessaries of life. Well, if that statement be true, it means that 4,000,000 of the inhabitants of these islands are without visible means of subsistence, not because of any fault on their part, but because our present land and industrial system denies them the opportunity of working for a living. In London alone it is estimated by those best able to form a judgment that 50,000 men are unemployed. This does not refer to those who are casually employed, and it does not refer to those usually spoken of as loafers and criminals. It refers exclusively to bona fide working men who have been thrown out of employment in consequence of bad trade.

We have in addition to these – and I trust the House will admit it to be our duty to legislate even in the interest of the loafer and the criminal – we have in addition to these figures 300,000 who are classed as casual workers – as loafers and criminals – men whose earnings are intermittent and under 18s. per week. These figures, let me say again, refer to London alone. In addition to these, we have close on 400,000 whose earnings are under 21s. per week. In Liverpool the number of men unemployed who have reported themselves is 7,000; in Glasgow 15,000; in Hull 6,000; in Birmingham 5,000; in Sunderland 4,000; in Derby 2,000; in Stockton 1,500. I think, Sir, that these men have a right to look to this House for assistance in finding employment.

It was stated in the House yesterday that the laws of this country permitted manufactures to be brought into the country from wherever they could he produced with the greatest cheapness. I admit that is so, and I do not object to its being so; but I submit that if the laws of this country are so framed as to throw men out of employment it is the duty of this House to enable these men to provide themselves with the means of subsistence. Can that be done? Remember that this question not only affects those out-of-work, but also those workers who are in employment.

I believe all the horrors of sweating, of low wages, of long hours, and of deaths from starvation, are directly traceable to the large numbers of people who are totally unemployed or only casually employed. The worker in the workshop is fettered by the thought that outside his workshop gates there are thousands eager and willing to step into his shoes should he be dismissed in consequence of any attempt to improve his position.

I therefore submit that in dealing with the problem of the unemployed we are dealing with the whole industrial problem, and those who object to long hours being limited by Act of Parliament should at least aid us in providing means for the absorption of the unemployed in order to give the workers employed a free hand in shortening the hours of labour without the aid of the Legislature.

I know that the difficulty is to find a remedy for what everyone admits to be an evil of no little magnitude. Quite a number of remedies have been proposed and discussed. Amongst others, emigration long held the field; but it has been found that emigration is not a cure for the evil, that emigration sends out of the country the best part of our working classes – the thrifty, prudent, sober and intelligent workers, the very men whom we desire to keep at home; and that we get in exchange for them the Jew, the poor degraded workers of the Continent, who come here to fill the vacuum left by our own people who leave our shores. But even emigration will not long avail as a remedy. America with all its broad acres is closing the door as rapidly as it may against the immigrant from all lands, and what is true of that land is true of many others.

It may be said, however, that there is plenty of room in Canada. But in the Canadian industrial centres the unemployed problem exists as well as here, and if there is plenty of room in Canada it would be well for Canada to settle her own unemployed problem. It is also said that a turn for the better in trade will again absorb the unemployed.

But I ask, is it right for this House, representing as it is supposed to do every section of the community, to coldly stand by, waiting for the return of good trade, while men, women and children are literally starving to death? Our present Poor Law system aggravates, but does not enable us to grapple with the evil, and it is not human to expect that the men who are suffering will suffer in silence, waiting for the return of good trade. Then it has been suggested by, amongst others, the President of the Local Government Board, that the increase of municipal activity would help to relieve the distress now prevailing. I admit that it would do so; but the response to the circular issued by the Local Government Board has not been encouraging enough to justify any high expectations being founded on this movement, and, besides, it is not fair to assume that municipal activity should be spasmodic in its operation, and should depend upon the prevalence of bad trade. We want municipal activity all the year round, and even then it will be found that there will be no lack of workers to meet any increased demand for labour.

My Amendment has been objected to because it contains no specific proposal for dealing with the evil. Had it done so, it would have been objected to still more, because then I am certain that everyone who wanted to find an excuse for not voting for the Amendment would find it in the proposal it contained. I think the House will agree with me that we have a high authority in this House for not disclosing the details of our proposals until we are in a position to give effect to them, which is not quite in my power yet. I wish to say that I have no sympathy with, and no intention of supporting, any proposal for dealing with the unemployed question which means a return to Protection. I want to make that perfectly clear, in order to remove excuses behind which certain Members intend to shelter themselves when we come to vote on this Amendment. I would resist as strongly as any Member of this House any attempt to again impose Protection in any shape or form on the trade and commerce of our country. It would aggravate every social and industrial evil and divert the minds of the workers from what I believe to be the true solution of this problem.

But whilst abstaining from making any specific proposal in my Amendment, I wish to enumerate one or two things which the Government might do in order to immediately relieve some of the distress now prevailing. The Government is a very large employer of labour. It has its dockyards, its arsenals, and its other departments in which large numbers of workers are employed. I have had occasion recently to go amongst the workers in several of these departments, and I heard the gravest complaints made against the system of overtime which is allowed to prevail in the Government Departments. There are two reforms which the workers in these departments demand and which, if established, would bring credit to the Government and be a slight step in the direction of solving the problem of the unemployed. First, there is the increase of the minimum wage for labourers to sixpence an hour; and, secondly, the enactment of a 48-hour week for all Government employees. It may be said that the workers do not desire these reforms, and that it is not the duty of the Government to force them upon the workers.

I hold in my hand a copy of a Petition addressed to the Lords Commissioners of the Admiralty by the workers under their control, and amongst the demands made in that Petition are the following: – We pray your Lordships to abolish the system of overtime, and to allow extra time only to he worked in cases of emergency. We pray your Lordships to reduce the hours of labour to 48 per week by closing the workshops at 12 o'clock noon on Saturdays.

Then again, there is the question of keeping contracts for Government work at home. This House is under an obligation in that matter despite the answer given by the First Lord of the Treasury in reply to a question addressed to him on the Friday of last week; for by a Resolution passed in this House on the 13th February, 1891, it was declared to be the duty of the Government in all Government contracts to make provision against sweating and all necessary conditions, to prevent the abuses arising front subletting of work, and to ensure the payment of the wages current in each trade for competent workers. I submit to the Government that it is not consistent with the spirit of that Resolution to go to Bavaria, or anywhere else outside Great Britain, for the supplies of the Post Office. The Government have no means of ascertaining whether this Resolution has been applied on the part of the firms with whom they deal abroad. Dealing with firms at home they would know whether the terms of the Resolution were enforced; and if they were not enforced, they would know how to apply the remedy. But when they go with their work to other lands, they pass beyond the sphere of their own influence, and are powerless to carry out the spirit of the Resolution. If the Government got their supplies at house, additional employment would also be given to our own people in the production of those supplies. Then there is the case of the Post Office, where there have been many reforms, but where there is room for many more reforms in the direction of shortening the hours of labour and employing extra workers.

Then there is a consensus of opinion that the time is ripe for dealing with the hours of labourers on railways, on tramways, and labourers engaged in modes of transit generally. It has been estimated by competent authorities that were the hours of railway servants reduced to eight per day employment would he found for 150,000 additional working men, and that surely is an item worthy of being taken into consideration by the Government.

The Government might also establish what is known as home colonies on the idle lands about which we have heard so much discussion in this House. This is not a question of theory, for it has been tried with the most satisfactory results. I do not refer to the penal and beggar colonies established by some Continental countries; I refer to what has been tried at home. Some years ago, at Newcastle, the Board of Guardians made provision for finding employment for the paupers in the workhouse. They were the ordinary class of paupers, belonging to all trades and occupations, and to no special trade or occupation. The Guardians set them to work, first to pull down and rebuild the workhouse, which they did to the satisfaction of all concerned; and afterwards the paupers were set to making their own clothing and everything necessary for carrying on the workhouse. A Report was made on the experiment, which stated that in every department it was found that the production was far more than the house needed. 'Everything', said the Report, 'in the house is made – from an ambulance to a the plate.' The Guardians also put into cultivation 14 acres or land in their possession, with such good results that the net profit on the sale of the produce in three years was £338. If the Guardians of Newcastle could do this, is it not reasonable to suppose that every Board of Guardians in Great Britain could do the same in their own locality? There is no lack of vacant land – land capable of producing for the people who are starving; and I submit that this House, as representing the nation, should give these men who are out of work the opportunity of employing themselves through this system of home colonisation. It would prevent the fearful demoralisation which being out of work never fails to bring in its train.

One of the most harrowing features connected with the problem of the unemployed is not the poverty or the hardship they have to endure, but the fearful moral degradation that follows in the train of the enforced idleness; and there is no more pitiable spectacle in this world than the man willing to work, who, day after day, vainly begs a brother of the earth to give him leave to toil. I am anxious that the Government should have the fullest opportunity of getting to work with their legislative proposals, and I hope that one of them will include something at least being done for the unemployed, because I would again point out that this is not merely making provision for men out of work during periods of bad trade. In every season of the year, and in every condition of trade, men are unemployed. The pressure under which industry is carried on to-day necessitates that the young and the strong and the able should have preference in obtaining employment; and if the young, the strong, and the able are to have the preference, then the middle-aged and the aged are of necessity thrown out upon the streets.

We are now discussing an Address of Thanks to Her Majesty for Her Speech. I want to ask the Government what have the unemployed to thank Her Majesty for in the Speech which has been submitted to the House? Their ease is overlooked and ignored; they are left out as if they did not exist. Their misery and their sufferings could not be greater, but there is no mention of them in the Queen's Speech. I take it that this House is the mouthpiece of the nation as a whole, and that it should speak for the nation – for the unemployed equally as for the well-to-do classes. But this House will not be speaking in the name of the nation, but only in the name of a section of the nation, if something is not done, and done speedily, for those people whose sufferings are so great, and for whom I plead.

I observe that a certain section of what are called the London Liberal Members have declared their intention of voting against this Amendment. They are, of course, free so to do; but I promise them a full exchange value for the vote they will give against the Amendment. I would remind the Government, too, that what lost them Huddersfield was the absence of the unemployed question from their Programme, and the absence of a candidate in sympathy with labour; and unless they desire the experience of Huddersfield to be repeated in the various constituencies where vacancies now exist, they would do well to give heed to a question which is so pressing as the one we are now engaged in discussing.

I am sure that if the election addresses and election promises of gentlemen on both sides of the House were examined, it would be found that during election contests they had plenty of professions of sympathy for the unemployed. I ask of them today that they should translate these professions into practice. It is said that this Amendment amounts to a Vote of Want of Confidence in the Government, and that, therefore, Hon. Members opposite will not vote for it. The Government that does not legislate for the unemployed does not deserve the confidence of this House; and Members representing London constituencies will take care not to go to their constituencies with these arguments on their lips. If the Queen's Speech contained any reference to this question of anything like a satisfactory nature, I would not have raised it on the present occasion; but having raised it, I will, as I have said, take the sense of the House upon it. It may be pointed out to me that the Queen's Speech does contain promises of many great and useful measures. That may be so; but if the Queen's Speech did not contain an allusion to the question of Home Rule, we should have an Amendment proposed protesting against that omission. The unemployed number 4,000,000, which is nearly equal to the population of Ireland, and am I to be told that a question affecting 4,000,000 people – affecting, not only their patriotism, or their comfort, but affecting their very lives – is of less consequence than the question of Home Rule for Ireland? And if the Hon. Gentlemen who represent the cause of Nationalism in Ireland would have felt justified in risking the life of the Government on the question of Home Rule, I claim to be more than justified in taking a similar risk in the interests of the unemployed. I beg, Mr Speaker, to move my Amendment.

'...the sunshine of socialism and human freedom...'

APPENDIX 2

The speech given by Keir Hardie in Bradford on
11 April 1914 to mark the 21st anniversary of the
formation of the Independent Labour Party

I SHALL NOT weary you by repeating the tale of how public opinion has changed during those 21 years. But, as an example, I may recall the fact that in those days, and for many years thereafter, it was tenaciously upheld by the public authorities, here and elsewhere, that it was an offence against laws of nature and ruinous to the State for public authorities to provide food for starving children, or independent aid for the aged poor. Even safety regulations in mines and factories were taboo. They interfered with the 'freedom of the individual'. As for such proposals as an eight-hour day, a minimum wage, the right to work and municipal houses, any serious mention of such classed a man as a fool.

These cruel, heartless dogmas, backed up by quotations from Jeremy Bentham, Malthus and Herbert Spencer, and by a bogus interpretation of Darwin's theory of evolution, were accepted as part of the unalterable laws of nature, sacred and inviolable, and were maintained by statesmen, town councillors, ministers of the Gospel, and, strangest of all, by the bulk of trade union leaders. That was the political, social and religious element in which our party saw the light. There was much bitter fighting in those days. Even municipal contests evoked the wildest passions. And if today there is a kindlier social atmosphere it is mainly because of 21 years' work of the ILP.

Scientists are constantly revealing the hidden powers of nature. By the aid of the x-rays we can now see through rocks and stones; the discovery of radium has revealed a great force which is already healing disease and will one day drive machinery; Marconi, with his wireless system of telegraphy and now of telephony, enables us to speak and send messages for thousands of miles through space.

Another discoverer, through means of the same invisible medium, can blow up ships, arsenals, and forts at a distance of eight miles.

But though these powers and forces are only now being revealed, they have existed since before the foundation of the world. The scientists, by sympathetic study and laborious toil, have brought them within our ken. And so, in like manner, our socialist propaganda is revealing hidden and hitherto undreamed-of powers and forces in human nature.

Think of the thousands of men and women who, during the past 21 years, have toiled unceasingly for the good of the race. The results are already being seen on every hand, alike in legislation and administration. And who shall estimate or put a limit to the forces and powers which yet lie concealed in human nature?

Frozen and hemmed in by a cold, callous greed, the warming influence of socialism is beginning to liberate them. We see it in the growing altruism of trade unionism. We see it, perhaps, most of all in the awakening of women. Who that has ever known woman as mother or wife has not felt the dormant powers which, under the emotions of life, or at the stern call of duty are even now momentarily revealed? And who is there who can even dimly forecast the powers that lie latent in the patient drudging woman, which a freer life would bring forth? Woman, even more than the working class, is the great unknown quantity of the race.

Already we see how their emergence into politics is affecting the prospects of men. Their agitation has produced a state of affairs in which even radicals are afraid to give more votes to men, since they cannot do so without also enfranchising women. Henceforward we must march forward as comrades in the great struggle for human freedom.

The Independent Labour Party has pioneered progress in this country, is breaking down sex barriers and class barriers, is giving a lead to the great women's movement as well as to the great working-class movement. We are here beginning the 22nd year of our existence. The past 21 years have been years of continuous progress, but we are only at the beginning. The emancipation of the worker has still to be achieved and just as the ILP in the past has given a good, straight lead, so shall the ILP in the future, through good report and through ill, pursue the even tenor of its way, until the sunshine of socialism and human freedom break forth upon our land.

'What is the cause of the war?'

APPENDIX 3

Keir Hardie's speech to the anti-war meeting in Trafalgar Square on 2 August 1914, as reported in the *Daily Citizen*[1]

WE HAVE MET to protest against the crime of war and bloodshed. Tonight there are millions of hearts in every country in Europe filled with sadness and foreboding. What is the cause of the war? You have no quarrel with Germany. German workmen have no quarrel with their French comrades. The French worker has no quarrel with his Austrian comrades. If that be so, why are we on the verge of the greatest calamity Europe has even seen?

We are told that there are international treaties which compel us to take part. Who made those treaties? The people had no voice in them. Are we going to allow Courts and the ruling classes to make treaties leading us into war without our having a word to say? We should not be in this position but for our alliance with Russia. Friends and comrades, this very square has rung with denunciations of Russian atrocities. Surely if there is one country under the sun which we ought to have no agreement with it is the foul government of anti-democratic Russia.

I ask again: What can we do? We can say to our government and to our King that we, the working classes of England will not have war. Italy is as much involved by treaty as we are, and yet Italy has decided to stand neutral. Why cannot Great Britain do the same? We are not defending our shores, which are not being attacked. We are not defending our liberties, which are not being menaced. We are here to say that in so far as we can there shall be no shot fired, no sabre drawn, in this war of conquest.

The only class which can prevent the Government going to war is the working class.

Endnotes

Introduction

1   Hughes, E (ed), *Keir Hardie's Speeches and Writings*, Forward, Glasgow, 1928.

2   Brown, G, *Maxton,* Fontana, Glasgow, 1988.

3   Connolly, J, *Workers' Republic,* 2 October 1915.

4   Morgan, KO, *Keir Hardie: Radical and Socialist*, Phoenix, London, 1997.

5   *Ibid.*

6   Hughes, E (ed), 1928.

7   Nevin, D, *James Connolly: A Full Life,* Gill and Macmillan, Dublin, 2014.

8   Smith, K, 'Understanding Keir Hardie and what he meant by Cumnock Time', *The Herald,* 2 June 2015.

CHAPTER 1 Socialism: More than a Creed

1   Quoted in the Independent Labour Party, Glasgow Federation, Keir Hardie Memorial Service Souvenir Programme, September 1919.

2   *Ibid.*

3   Stewart, W, *The Life of J Keir Hardie*, ILP, London 1946.

4   Callow, J (ed), *From Serfdom to Socialism*, Lawrence & Wishart, London, 2015; Hughes, E, *Keir Hardie*, George Allen and Unwin, London, 1956.

5   Callow, J, 2015.

6   Benn, C, *Keir Hardie*, Random House, London, 1992.

7   Hughes, E, 1956.

8   Martin, K, *Harold Laski: A Biography*, Jonathan Cape, London, 1969.

9   Williams, R, *Keywords*, Fontana Press, London, 1983.

10 *Kilmarnock Herald*, 1 January 1892, National Library of Scotland.

11 Tracey, H (ed), *The Book of the Labour Party Volume I*, Caxton, London, 1925

12 Callow, J, 2015.

13 MacArthur, B (ed), *The Penguin Book of Twentieth Century Speeches*, Penguin Books, 1999.

14 Tracey, H (ed), *The Book of the Labour Party Volume III*, Caxton, London, 1925.

15 Callow, J, 2015.

16 *Ibid.*

17 *Ibid.*

18 *Ibid.*

19 Tracey, H (ed), Volume I, 1925.

20 Letter from Hardie to son James, 19 September 1913, in the private collection of Dolores May Arias.

21 Callow, J, 2015.

22 *Ibid.*

23 Postcard from James Keir Hardie to Andrew Fisher, 14 December 1907, National Library of Australia Digital Collections.

24 Johnson, F, *Keir Hardie's Socialism*, ILP, London, 1922

25 Callow, J, 2015

26 Callow, J, 2015.

CHAPTER 2 Christianity: Christian and Socialist

1 Holman, B, *Keir Hardie: Labour's Greatest Hero*, Lion Hudson, Oxford, 2010.

2 Stewart, W, *J Keir Hardie,* Independent Labour Party, London, 1921.

3 McLean, I, *Keir Hardie,* Allen Lane, London, 1975.

4 Morgan, KO, *Keir Hardie, Prophet and Pioneer,* Weidenfeld and Nicolson, London, 1984 (first published 1975).

5 Cole, M, *Makers of the Labour Movement,* Longman, Green and Co, London, 1948.

6 Smout, TC, *A Century of the Scottish People 1830–1950,* Collins, London, 1986.

7 Lowe, D, *From Pit to Parliament: The Story of the Early Life of James Keir Hardie,* Labour Publishing Co, London, 1933.

8 Hardie, K, *From Serfdom to Socialism,* George Allen, London, 1907.

9 Holman, B, 2010.

10 *Ibid.*

11 Hughes, E, (ed.), *Keir Hardie's Speeches and Writings,* Forward Printing and Publishing Co, London, 1928.

12 Brown, G, in his Introduction to Bob Holman, *Keir Hardie: Labour's Greatest Hero?,* Lion Hudson, Oxford, new edition, 2015.

13 Hughes, H (ed), 1928.

14 Holman, B, 2010.

15 Stewart, W, *J Keir Hardie,* Independent Labour Party, London, 1921.

16 Hughes, E (ed), 1928.

17 Holman, B, 2010.

18 *Ibid.*

19 *Ibid.*

20 *Ibid.*

21   Holman, B, 2010.

22   *Ibid.*

CHAPTER 3 International Peace: A Legacy for the Peace Movement

1   Stewart, W, *J Keir Hardie*, ILP, London, 1921.

2   *Hansard*, 17 March 2003, column 728.

3   Griffiths, G, *Henry Richard: Apostle of Peace and Welsh Patriot*, Francis Boutle, London, 2012.

4   Morgan, KO, *Keir Hardie: Radical and Socialist*, Weidenfeld and Nicolson, London, 1975.

CHAPTER 4 Trade Unionism: Independent Labour Representation

1   Williams, F, *Magnificent Journey: The Rise of the Trade Unions*, Oldham Press, London, 1954.

2   Knox, WWJ, *Industrial Nation: Work, Culture and Society in Scotland, 1800–Present*, Edinburgh University Press, Edinburgh, 1999.

3   Campbell, A, *The Scottish Miners 1874–1939*, vol II: *Trade Unions and Politic*, Ashgate Publishing Ltd, Aldershot, 2000.

4   *Ardrossan and Saltcoats Herald*, 24 June 1882.

5   Campbell, A, 2000.

6   Williams, F, 1954.

7   Reid, F, *Keir Hardie: The Making of a Socialist*, Croom Helm, 1978.

8   Hardie, K, 'A Friendly Chat with the Scotch Miners', *Labour Leader*, 20 October 1894.

9   Burns, J, *The Liverpool Congress 1890*, quoted in Pelling, H, *Origins of the Labour Party 1880–1900*, Oxford University Press, Oxford, 1965.

10   Williams, F, 1954.

11   See Knox, *Industrial Nation*, for a fuller analysis of these issues.

12   Williams, F, 1954.

13   See Joyce, P, *Work, Society and Politics: The Culture of the Factory in Late Victorian England*, Harvester Press, Brighton, 1980 for a discussion of this phenomenon.

14   Williams, F, 1954.

15   Pelling, H, 1965.

16   Howell, D, *British Workers and the ILP 1888–1906*, Manchester University Press, Manchester, 1983.

17   *Ibid.*

18   Williams, F, 1954.

19 *Ibid.*

20 *Ibid.*

21 Reid, AJ, *United We Stand: A History of Britain's Trade Unions*, Allen Lane, London, 2004.

22 Reid, *United*, Williams, *Magnificent Journey*.

23 Harvie, C, 'Before the Breakthrough, *1888–1922*', in *Forward! Labour Politics in Scotland 1888–1988*, ed. Donnachie, I *et al*, Polygon, Edinburgh, 1989.

24 Pelling, H, 1965.

25 Cole, GDH, *A History of the Labour Party from 1914*, Routledge and Kegan Paul, London 1948.

26 Morgan, K, *Keir Hardie: Radical and Socialist*, Weidenfeld and Nicolson, London, 1975.

27 Ray Collins, *Building a One Nation Labour Party: Interim Report*, Labour Party, London, 2013.

28 Pelling, H, 1965.

CHAPTER 5 The ILP: Keir Hardie, Evangelist and Strategist

1 Winslow, C (ed), EP Thompson and the Making of the New Left 'Homage to Tom Maguire', Lawrence & Wishart Ltd, London, 2014, and to be published as a pamphlet by the ILP.

2 Benn, C, *Keir Hardie*, Richard Cohen Books, London, 1997.

3 Howell, D, Br*itish Workers and the Independent Labour Party, 1888–1906*, Manchester University Press, Manchester, 1983.

4 McBriar, AM, *Fabian Socialism and English Politics 1884–1918*, Cambridge University Press, Cambridge, 1962.

5 Morgan, KO, *Labour's Greatest Hero: Keir Hardie*, Weidenfeld and Nicholson, London, 2008.

6 Benn, 1997.

7 Brockway, F, *Inside the Left*, Oxford University Press, Oxford, 2004 edition.

CHAPTER 6 Women's Suffrage: Unfailing Support

1 Pankhurst, S, *The Home Front*, Hutchinson and Co Ltd, London, 1932.

2 Benn, C, *Keir Hardie*, Hutchinson, London, 1997.

3 Pankhurst, S, *The Suffragette Movement*, Wharton Press, reprinted 2010.

4 *Ibid.*

5 Benn, 1997.

6 *Ibid.*

7   *Hansard*, 29 March 1928.

8   Pankhurst, 2010.

9   *Ibid.*

10   Morgan, KO, *Keir Hardie, Radical and Socialist,* Weidenfeld and Nicholson, London, 1975.

11   *Votes for Women*, 1 October 1909.

12   *Ibid.*

13   *The Suffragette*, October 1912.

14   Smyth, E, *Female Pipings in Eden*, P Davies, London, 1934.

15   *Labour Leader*, 30 September 1915

CHAPTER 7 Home Rule: Socialist, Not Nationalist

1   Holman, B, *Keir Hardie: Labour's Greatest Hero?*, Lion Hudson, Oxford, 2010.

2   Brown, G, *My Scotland, Our Britain*, Simon and Shuster, London, 2014.

3   Kenefick, W, *Red Scotland!*, Edinburgh University Press, Edinburgh, 2007.

4   Knox, W, *Industrial Nation*, Edinburgh University Press, Edinburgh, 1999.

5   Hughes, E, *Keir Hardie*, Lincolns-Prager, London, 1950.

6   Kenefick, 2007.

7   Keating, M and Bleiman, D, *Labour and Scottish Nationalism*, Macmillan, London 1979.

8   Keating and Bleiman, 1979.

9   *Ibid.*

10   Hardie, JK, *From Serfdom to Socialism*, George Allen, London, 1907.

11   Finlay, R, essay in *The Modern SNP: From Protest to Power*, Edinburgh University Press, Edinburgh, 2009.

12   Benn, C, *Keir Hardie*, Richard Cohen Books, London, 1997.

13   *Ibid.*

14   Morgan, KO, *Keir Hardie: Radical and Socialist*, Weidenfeld and Nicholson, London, 1975.

15   Holman,B, *Why Ed Miliband Should Learn the Lessons of Keir Hardie, Herald,* 12 September 2014.

16   Devine, T, *The Scottish Nation 1700–2000*, Allen Lane, London, 1999.

17   Quoted in Mills and others, *Myths, Realties, Radical Future*, Red Paper Collective, Glasgow, 2015.

18   Campbell, S, *Keir Hardie's Grave*, Wings over Scotland 2014 http://wingsover-scotland.com/keir-hardies-grave/ and Labour voters for independence, *Would Keir*

Hardie be spinning in his grave? https://www.facebook.com/labourforindepend-
ence/posts/10200552680019680.

19 *Daily Record* 5 May 2015.

CHAPTER 8 West Ham: 'A Splotch of Red'

1   Hughes, E (ed.), *Keir Hardie's Speeches and Writings, from 1888 to 1915,*
    Forward Printing and Publishing Company, Glasgow, *c.* 1928, C. Benn, C *Keir,
    Hardie,* Richard Cohen Books, London, 1992 rpt. 1997, Cockburn, J, *The Hungry
    Heart: A Romantic Biography of James Keir Hardie,* Jarrolds, London, 1956,
    and Morgan, KO, *Keir Hardie: Radical and Socialist,* Weidenfeld and Nicolson,
    London, 1975.

2   Fyfe, H, *Keir Hardie,* Duckworth, London, 1935.

3   Claisse, J, *Will Thorne, The Campaign for West Ham South, 1906,* BA thesis,
    University of Manchester, 1982, J. Lewis, J, *East Ham and West Ham Past,*
    Historical Publications, London, 2004, McDougall, D (ed.), *Fifty Years a
    Borough, 1886–1936,* County Borough of West Ham, London, 1936, and Tully, J,
    *Silvertown, The Lost Story of a Strike that Shook London and Helped Launch the
    Modern Labor Movement,* Monthly Review Press, New York, 2014.

4   Quoted in: Claisse, J, *Will Thorne.*

5   Cunninghame Graham quoted in: Anon, *Presentation and Unveiling of Bust of
    J Keir Hardie,* MP for West Ham South, *1892–95 at the West Ham Town Hall,
    Stratford, E15, Tuesday 20th January 1948,* National Labour Press, London, 1948.

6   Claisse, J, 1982 and McDougall (ed.), 1936.

7   Powell, WR, *Keir Hardie in West Ham. A Constituency with a Past,* Socialist
    History Society, London, 2004.

8   Thompson, P, *Socialists, Liberals and Labour: The Struggle for London, 1885–
    1914,* Routledge and Kegan Paul, London, 1967.

9   Morgan, KO, 1975; McDougall (ed.), 1936; Tsuzuki,C, *HM Hyndman and
    British Socialism,* Oxford University Press, Oxford, 1961, and Tully, *Silvertown.*

10 Powell, WR, 2004; Benn, C, 1997.

11 Keir Hardie, quoted in: Anon, *Presentation and Unveiling of Bust of J Keir Hardie.*

12 Morgan, KO, 1975; Powell, WR, 2004; and Moore, R,*The Emergence of the
    Labour Party, 1880–1924,* Hodder and Stoughton, London, Sydney, Auckland and
    Toronto, 1978.

13 *Ibid.*

14 *Ibid.*

15 *Ibid.*

16 Morgan, KO, 1975; Powell, WR, 2004; Hughes, E (ed.) 1928; Benn, C, 1997.

17 Washington, Samuel,*Workman's Times,* 11 February 1893, quoted in Hughes,
    Keir Hardie.

18 Thompson, *Socialists, Liberals and Labour*, Cole, GDH, *James Keir Hardie*, Fabian Society / Victor Gollancz Ltd., London, 1941, and Maxton, J, *Keir Hardie: Prophet and Pioneer*, Francis Johnson, London, c.1939.

19 Hughes, E (ed.) 1928.

20 Benn, C, 1997.

21 Powell, WR, 2004.

22 McDougall (ed.), *Fifty Years a Borough*,; Powell, WR, 2004; Benn, C, 1997; Stewart, 1928; *J Keir Hardie*, Hughes, E (ed.), 1928; and McLean, *Keir Hardie*, Allen Lane, London, 1975.

23 *Stratford Express*, June 1895, quoted in: Powell, WR, 2004.

24 Hughes, E (ed.), 1928.

25 Smith, F, *From Pit to Parliament: Keir Hardie's Life Story*, The People's Press, Stockport, 1909.

26 McDougall (ed.), *Fifty Years a Borough*, Anon. 'Our Representative Will Thorne', *The Social Democrat. A Monthly Socialist Review*, Twentieth Century Press, London, 1899, Vol. III no.12, and Claisse, *Will Thorne*.

27 Stewart, W, *J Keir Hardie*, ILP, London, 1921 and JB Glasier, *Keir Hardie: The Man and His Message*, ILP, London, 1919

CHAPTER 9 Merthyr Tydfil: Hardie's Welsh Odyssey

1   Hardie was an enthusiastic attendee at spiritualist meetings and séances in South Wales, notably at Abercynon in his constituency, where fellow enthusiasts claimed he returned some 30 years after his death to offer advice to the post-war Labour government.

2   Pelling, H: *Origins of the Labour Party*, Clarendon Press, London, 1954

3   Hughes, E, *Keir Hardie's Speeches and Writings*, ILP, London, 1928

4   *Labour Leader* newspaper, 7 July 1894 – quoted in Martin Wright's excellent PHD study of 'Wales and Socialism', Cardiff University. I owe Martin a great debt of gratitude as much of the original source material I quote was unearthed by him and many of the insights I draw lean heavily on his observations.

5   LP NAC Minutes 12 April 1898, quoted in Martin Wright op. cit.

6   Bevan, A, *In Place of Fear*, William Heinemann Ltd, London, 1952.

7   Quoted in Llewelyn Davies *Keir Hardie and the Harry Morris Memorial Meeting Programme*, 1926.

8   Morgan, K, *Labour People*, OUP, Oxford, 1987.

9   Keir Hardie 1906 Election Address, quoted in Martin Wright op. cit.

10 John Littlejohns, Llais Llafur 14 and 21 February 1902, quoted in Martin Wright op. cit.

CHAPTER 10 Cumnock: A Lasting Legacy

1   Stewart,W, *J Keir Hardie*, ILP, London, 1921.

2   http://www.electricscotland.com/history/hardie/chapter02.htm

3   Stewart, W, 1921.

4   Stead, WT, *Coming Men on Coming Questions*, No: VI, May, 18, 1905

CHAPTER 11 An Agitator: The Enduring Principle of Agitation

1   Benn, C, *Keir Hardie*, Hutchinson, London, 1992.

2   http://www.heraldscotland.com/comment/columnists/agenda.25275697

3   Morgan, K, 'Labour's Greatest Hero: Keir Hardie', *Guardian*, September 19 2008

4   *Ibid.*

5   Benn, C, 1992.

6   *Ibid.*

7   http://labourlist.org/2010/07/david-milibands-keir-hardie-lecture-full-speech/

8   Benn, C, 1992.

9   *Ibid.*

10 *Ibid.*

11 *Ibid.*

12 Paxman, J, *On Royalty*, Penguin, London, 2006.

13 http://spartacus-educational.com/PRhardie.htm

14 Benn, C, 1992.

15 *Ibid.*

16 http://spartacus-educational.com/PRhardie.htm

17 http://labourlist.org/2010/07/david-milibands-keir-hardie-lecture-full-speech/

APPENDIX 1

1   Plaut, M, *Keir Hardie in South Africa*. https://hatfulofhistory.wordpress.com 16 August 2014.

APPENDIX 3

1   Hughes, E (ed), *Keir Hardie's Speeches and Writings*, Forward, Glasgow, 1928.

Opening Quotes – References

CHAPTER 1

'*Socialism implies the inherent equality of all human beings.*'
From *Serfdom to Socialism*, Lawrence & Wishart, reprint, London, 2015.

CHAPTER 2

'*any system of production or exchange which sanctions the exploitation of the weak by the strong or the unscrupulous is wrong and therefore sinful.*'
Hardie, K, 'The Church and the Labour Problem' in *The Thinker: A Review of World-wide Christian Thought*, vol 3, 1898. Reprint, Forgotten Books, 2013.

CHAPTER 3

'*The angel of death with blood-stained wings is hovering over Europe.*'
Merthyr Pioneer, 25 July 1914.

CHAPTER 4

'*Socialism supplies the vision and a united working class satisfies the senses as a practical method of attaining its realisation.*'
Hardie, quoted in Johnson, F, *Keir Hardie's Socialism*; ILP, London, 1922.

CHAPTER 5

'*to secure the collective ownership of the means of production, distribution and exchange*'
The founding aims of the ILP, adopted in 1893 under the leadership of Keir Hardie.

CHAPTER 6

'*The "half angel, half idiot" period is over in the woman's world. She is fighting her way into every sphere of human activity.*'
Hardie, K: *The Citizenship of the World: A Please for Women's Suffrage*, ILP, London, 1906.

CHAPTER 7

'*The most we can hope to do is to make the coming of Socialism possible in the full assurance that it will shape itself aright when it does come.*'
Hardie, 1907.

CHAPTER 8

'*My first concern is the moral and material well-being of the working classes.*'
Hardie, K, Election Address, West Ham, 1892.

CHAPTER 9

'*Socialism is the natural faith of these people and it is catching on.*'
Hardie, K, Report from South Wales, *Labour Leader*, 25 June 1893.

CHAPTER 10

'*I am not specially anxious to go to Parliament, but I am anxious and determined that the wants and wishes of the working classes shall be made known and attended to there.*'
Hardie, quoted in Stewart, W, J *Keir Hardie*, ILP, London 1921.

CHAPTER 11

'*My work has consisted of trying to stir up a divine discontent with wrong.*'
Hardie, quoted in Benn, C, *Keir Hardie*, Hutchinson, London, 1992.

How to Join the Keir Hardie Society

Born in poverty in Legbrannock, near Holytown, North Lanarkshire, James Keir Hardie (1856–1915) had no formal education and was taught basic literacy by his mother. He took his first job at the age of seven and within three years he was working in a coal-mine.

With a strong sense of social justice and a vigorous appetite for self-education, he went on to become a leading figure in the labour movement, playing a major role in the formation of the Independent Labour Party and later the Labour Representation Committee, the forerunner of the present-day Labour Party. He served as a Member of Parliament for West Ham South (1892–95) and later for Merthyr Tydfil (1900–15).

The Keir Hardie Society was formed on 15 August 2010 and aims to keep alive the ideas and promote the life and work of Keir Hardie.

Membership is open to all who support the Society's objectives.

Annual membership per person is £10 waged / £4 unwaged.

Cheques should be made payable to the Keir Hardie Society.

To join the Keir Hardie Society please email: keirhardiesociety@gmail.com
or write to:

Richard Leonard, Keir Hardie Society, GMB Office, Fountain House, 1/3 Woodside Crescent, Glasgow G3 7UJ.

Find out more at **www.keirhardiesociety.co.uk**

Some other books published by **Luath Press**

Great Scottish Speeches Vol. I
Introduced and Edited by David Torrance
ISBN 978 1 906817 27 4 PBK £9.99

World in Chains – the impact of nuclear weapons and militarisation from a UK perspective
Angie Zelter
ISBN 978-1-910021-03-3 PBK £12.99

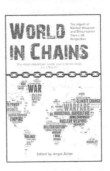

Some great Scottish speeches were the result of years of contemplation. Some flourished in heat of the moment. Whatever the background of the ideas expressed, the speeches not only provide a snapshot of their time, but express views that still resonate in Scotland today, whether you agree with the sentiments or not.

Encompassing speeches made by Scots or in Scotland, this carefully selected collection reveals the character of a nation. Themes of religion, independence and socialism cross paths with sporting encouragement, Irish Home Rule and Miss Jean Brodie.

Ranging from the legendary speech of the Caledonian chief Calgacus in 83AD right up to Alex Salmond's election victory in 2007, these are the speeches that created modern Scotland.

...what has not faded is the power of the written and spoken word – as this first-rate collection of Scottish speeches demonstrates.
PRESS AND JOURNAL

World in Chains is a collection of essays from well-reputed experts in their field, all of which deliver engaging and analytical critiques of nuclear warfare. They point to the changes needed to re-structure society, so that it is based on compassion, co-operation, love and respect for all. Their words inspire us to resist the growing militarisation and corporatisation of our world.

In the past I have often wondered why obviously unethical or inhumane horrors were able to take place, what people were doing at the time to prevent them or what kind of resistance was happening, how many people knew and tried to stop the genocide, slavery, poverty and pollution... I want those who come after my generation to know that, yes, we do know of the dangers of nuclear war, of climate chaos, of environmental destruction. This book will show you that there were many people working to change the structures that keep our world in chains. ANGIE ZELTER

Details of books published by Luath Press can be found at:
www.luath.co.uk

Luath Press Limited

committed to publishing well written books worth reading

LUATH PRESS takes its name from Robert Burns, whose little collie Luath (*Gael.*, swift or nimble) tripped up Jean Armour at a wedding and gave him the chance to speak to the woman who was to be his wife and the abiding love of his life. Burns called one of the 'Twa Dogs' Luath after Cuchullin's hunting dog in Ossian's *Fingal*. Luath Press was established in 1981 in the heart of Burns country, and is now based a few steps up the road from Burns' first lodgings on Edinburgh's Royal Mile. Luath offers you distinctive writing with a hint of unexpected pleasures.
Most bookshops in the UK, the US, Canada, Australia, New Zealand and parts of Europe, either carry our books in stock or can order them for you. To order direct from us, please send a £sterling cheque, postal order, international money order or your credit card details (number, address of cardholder and expiry date) to us at the address below. Please add post and packing as follows: UK – £1.00 per delivery address; overseas surface mail – £2.50 per delivery address; overseas airmail – £3.50 for the first book to each delivery address, plus £1.00 for each additional book by airmail to the same address. If your order is a gift, we will happily enclose your card or message at no extra charge.

Luath Press Limited
543/2 Castlehill
The Royal Mile
Edinburgh EH1 2ND
Scotland
Telephone: +44 (0)131 225 4326 (24 hours)
Fax: +44 (0)131 225 4324
email: sales@luath. co.uk
Website: www. luath.co.uk